Don't
OVER THINK

Building a happy life you Love

Dr.Y. Narasimha Raja

Ph.D., MBA, M.Sc. Psychology

Asst. Professor –School of Management,
Presidency University, Bengaluru

Email: ynraja.phd@gmail.com
Web: www.ynraja.com
Mob: +(91)8073205840

Dr. Y. Narasimha Raja

Copyrights Certification @ 2024
Don't Overthink – Building a happy life you love.
Dr. Y. Narasimha Raja & All rights reserved

MRP: Indian Rupees (INR) 160/-

Publishers: Notion Press

800, West El Camino Real #180,California USA 94040

Notion Press Media Pvt Ltd,

No.50, Chettiyar Agaram Main Road,Vanagaram, **Chennai, 600095, Contact +9144 46315631**

Email : publish@notionpress.com

web: www.notionpress.com

Index

Preface

A thousand disappointments in the past cannot equal the power of one Positive action right now. Go ahead and go for it. You dont have to be great to start. But you have to start to be great.

Overthinking is a pervasive issue in contemporary society, often hindering personal growth, happiness, and productivity. This book delves into the modern concepts of

✓ Causes of Overthinking
✓ Overcoming techniques to reduce overthinking
✓ The Impact of Overthinking
✓ Therapies
✓ Psychometric test & evaluation

This book provides a broad range of information concisely and in an easy-to-read manner. I assure you that if these principles are applied to your practical life situations, you will see positive results in a short span of time.

This book is written in simple language, it aims to empower readers through self-explanatory guidance and practical advice.

With you and for you

Dr. Y. Narasimha Raja

About Author -Dr. Y. Narasimha Raja

Dr. Y. Narasimha Raja multifaceted professional with significant contributions to the fields of Psychology, Management, and Human Resources. His extensive educational background, with a Ph.D. in Management Studies, and Master of Business Administration, Master of Science in Psychology and multiple master's degrees, complements his over 19 years of experience in corporate and academic sectors across India and internationally. As an award-winning HR practitioner and corporate trainer, Dr. Raja's expertise has been recognized by numerous prestigious awards.

Book Publications

1. Highly Effective Parenting Skills
2. Highly Effective Teaching Skills
3. The best & smart Teaching techniques
4. Happy Parenting Skills
5. Stage Fear
6. Highly effective Public Speaking Skills
7. Phobias-Overview on 165 phobias
8. Neuro Disorders
9. Counseling Skills
10. How to change life better?
11. Positive Psychology for a Successful people.
12. Don't Overthink

Dedicated
to the lovely Godess, my
Mother

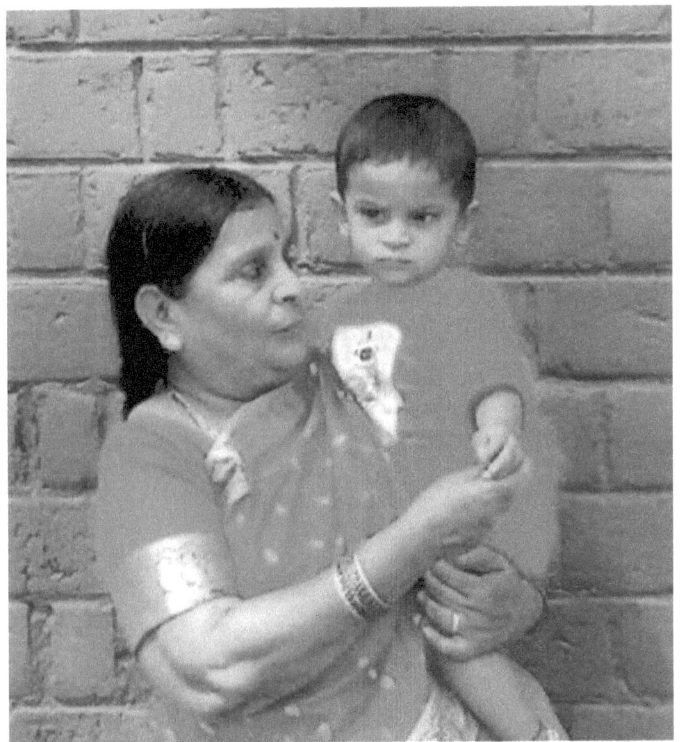

Mrs. Y. Rajeswari

Chapter-I
Hello to Over thinking

Overthinking is the biggest cause of our unhappiness. Keep yourself occupied. Keep your mind off things that don't help you. Be optimistic." - Roy T. Bennett

Overthinking refers to the process of thinking about a particular subject or situation excessively and for prolonged periods. This mental loop often results in an inability to focus on anything else, as the mind becomes consumed by the topic of concern. While it might seem beneficial to thoroughly analyze a problem from every possible angle, overthinking generally leads to negative outcomes, such as increased stress and reduced decision-making ability.

Have you ever watched a stone being thrown into a pond, Yes, and what happens? The stone disturbs the water and creates ripples. After some time, the ripples fade away and the pond returns to its calm state, that is like the mind. The stone is Overthinking. A single thought is like a stone thrown into the pond. If you throw stones continuously, the ripples will never settle. But if you allow them to, they eventually calm down. Similarly, if you keep indulging every thought, your mind will never find peace. stop overthinking.

Research findings about Overthinking

Research suggests that overthinking is associated with feelings of depression, anxiety, and post-traumatic stress disorder (PTSD)

In the book Who Think Too Much: How To Break Free of Overthinking and Reclaim Your Life," (2003, Henry Holt and Company). Among the findings" it's mentioned that overthinking is a big problem for many young and middle-aged adults. Surprisingly, it's less common among older adults

> ➢ Overthinking is a big problem for young and middle-aged adults in the country. About 73% of 25-35 year-olds think too much, while only 52% of 45-55 year-olds and 20% of 65-75 year-olds do.
> ➢ Women are more likely than men to overthink and get stuck because of it. About 57% of women and 43% of men overthink.

Overthinking can really mess with your happiness and mood. It's like making things worse in your head than they actually are. It's like creating problems that aren't even real. Overthinking makes us really unhappy. To feel better, try to stay busy and focus on things that make you feel good. Stay positive and don't worry too much about what could go wrong. Instead, think about what could go right!. Imagine overthinking is like sitting on a rocking chair. You're moving, but you're not going anywhere.

Overthinking and low EQ leads to endup life.

Genious legends , Nobel prize winners, Richesest business men, sinciests, celebrities etc also some times become overthinkers, end results they have not succeed to overcome from this Overthinking EQ. They have not judge the Emotions and situations properly.

Four Nobel Prize winners ended their lives due to overthinking.

Winning a Nobel Prize is a great achievement, showing exceptional knowledge and global recognition. Despite their brilliance, Nobel laureates like *Emil Fischer, Hans Fischer, Percy Bridgman, and Stanford Moore,* along with others like Ludwig Boltzmann, took their own lives. Overthinking may have been a factor. It reminds us that even the most accomplished individuals can struggle with mental health, emphasizing the importance of seeking support and balance in life.

The highest IQ multi billionaires committed sucide Low EQ

In our society, the pursuit of wealth is often intertwined with dreams and aspirations, with the belief that money can bring happiness and success. However, this narrative overlooks the complexities of human experience. The pressure to succeed can be overwhelming, leading to mental strain that manifests in various forms of stress, irrespective of circumstances. Tragically, even individuals with substantial financial resources are not immune to the challenges of mental health. Here are examples of successful businessmen who tragically took their own lives:

- ➤ Jonathan Wraith, a young British millionaire, unexpectedly ended his life, possibly overwhelmed by familial concerns.
- ➤ Eli M. Black, a Jewish-American businessman, faced ruin due to scandal, ending his life by jumping from his office building.
- ➤ Huibert Boumeester, a Dutch millionaire banker, succumbed to depression following a major corporate takeover, leaving behind a note expressing his despair.
- ➤ Christopher Foster, despite being a wealthy businessman, took his own life after financial troubles pushed him to a breaking point.
- ➤ John Lawrenson and his wife ended their lives together as she battled cancer, unable to face the prospect of life without her.
- ➤ Wayne Pai, a respected Taiwanese businessman, died amidst allegations of impropriety, leaving behind a cloud of suspicion.
- ➤ Paul Castle, a prominent figure in British society, took his own life amidst financial setbacks and personal struggles.
- ➤ Peter Smedley, a successful hotelier, chose to end his life due to severe illness, a decision documented by the BBC.

> ➢ Howard Worthington's life ended tragically after a violent incident, highlighting the destructive consequences of unchecked emotions.
> ➢ ReiJane Huai, a former CEO, ended his life following legal troubles, leaving behind a legacy of innovation overshadowed by tragedy.

These heartbreaking stories offer no immunity to the struggles of the human condition, underscoring the importance of mental health awareness and support.

The Highest IQ = EQ will contribute to lead the happy, relationship, social life successful life. This book is to identify the causes of overthinking, strategies to overcome and scientific methodologies that reader should overcome from the Overthinking and lead a life happlily.

Chapter-II
Causes of Overthinking

"The cause is hidden. The effect is visible to all." — Ovid

Understanding the cause of overthinking is crucial, as every effect stems from a specific cause. Recognizing the root cause of overthinking is the first step toward addressing and overcoming it. By identifying why we overthink, we can develop effective strategies to combat it and improve our mental well-being.

The major causes of overthinking is mentioned below:-

1. Free time is Devils time. Idle Hands Are the devil's playground

When you find yourself with free time and no work, it is devils mind, you start doing FOLLOWUPS, Whatsapp chats "How are you," eager to know others information and giving REMINDERS, Micromanagement, it's important to stay productive. Use this opportunity to engage in activities that enrich your life and contribute positively to your well-being. Whether it's pursuing hobbies, learning something new, volunteering, or taking care of tasks you've been putting off, staying busy can help you make the most of your time. By staying productive, you not only avoid boredom but also cultivate a sense of accomplishment and fulfillment. So, instead of letting idle time go to waste, seize the moment and make it meaningful by staying active and productive.

A proverb is a short saying that offers advice or wisdom. The proverb "idle hands are the devil's playground" means that when people have too much free time, they might end up doing bad things.

This saying is a warning to everyone, especially parents and teachers, to keep themselves and others busy with good activities. If people are not busy with meaningful work, they might fill their time with harmful behaviors.The idea that being lazy can lead to trouble has been around for a long time. In the 4th century, St. Jerome wrote, "Engage in some occupation, so that the devil may always find you busy," which is where the modern version of the proverb likely comes from.In simple terms, the proverb tells us that staying busy with good things helps keep us out of trouble. The Overthinkers they require a support and continuious interactions to overcome from their limitations.

"It is not that we have a short time to live, but that we waste a lot of it," Seneca. means that life feels short not because we actually have little time, but because we often waste it. When we overthink about others' matters, we spend too much time worrying about things we can't control. This makes us lose time that could be used for more important and enjoyable activities.

To overcome overthinking, focus on what you can control and let go of what you can't. Keep yourself busy with productive tasks and hobbies. Practice mindfulness by staying present in the moment, rather than getting lost in thoughts about others. Set aside specific times to reflect on things, but don't let it take over your entire day. Talk to someone you trust about your worries; sharing can help lighten the mental load.

Buddha has emphasised on time for the productive not for the overthinking is **"The trouble is, you think you have time,"** *means that people often believe they have plenty of time to do things, so they keep delaying. This can lead to procrastination and wasted opportunities.*

When related to overthinking, it suggests that we shouldn't spend too much time caught up in endless thoughts and worries. Overthinking can make us delay actions and miss out on living in the present. Instead of assuming we have all the time in the world, we should act now and focus on what's important, avoiding unnecessary overthinking.

Steve Jobs was a visionary entrepreneur, inventor, and co-founder of Apple Inc., one of the most successful and innovative technology companies in the world. He explain the secreat to his growth is importance of time not to overthink. **"Your time is limited, so don't waste it living someone else's life,"** means that we only have a limited amount of time in our lives, so we shouldn't spend it trying to be like someone else or doing what others expect us to do. Instead, we should focus on living our own lives to the fullest.

In simple terms, the message is not to waste time by being idle or worrying too much about what others think. Instead, use your time to pursue your own goals, dreams, and passions. Don't spend too much time trying to fit into someone else's idea of who you should be. Focus on being true to yourself and making the most of the time you have.

"When you arise in the morning, think of what a precious privilege it is to be alive – to breathe, to think, to enjoy, to love."

This quote from Marcus Aurelius, reminds us to appreciate life's simple blessings every day. Keeping Overthinking away, one can benefit from starting their day with gratitude, focusing on positive aspects rather than worrying about what might go wrong.

The key is in not spending time, but in investing it.

Instead of wasting time, Stephen R Covery's quote suggests that we should use our time wisely, like an investment. Overthinkers can learn to use their free time productively by engaging in activities that nourish their well-being or help them grow.

"Time heals what reason cannot."

This quote from the Senceca implies that time has the power to heal things that logic or reasoning cannot. Overthinkers can find solace in the fact that with time, their worries may fade and things may get better.

"Lost time is never found again."

Franklin's quote emphasizes the irretrievable nature of wasted time. Overthinkers can understand that spending too much time dwelling on things that don't matter is a loss they can't recover.

"The future depends on what you do today."

Gandhi's quote emphasizes the importance of present actions in shaping the future. Overthinkers can focus on taking small steps today rather than worrying excessively about what might happen tomorrow.

2. Gossip a tool for Overthinking

"Gossip is just a tool to distract people who have nothing better to do from feeling jealous of those few of us still remaining with noble hearts." - Anna Godbersen

Gossip is when people talk about others, often sharing personal or private information, rumors, or speculation. It's usually done in a casual or informal manner, and the information may or may not be true. Gossip can spread quickly through social circles, and it often involves discussing someone's behavior, relationships, or actions. While gossip can sometimes be harmless, it can also be hurtful or damaging, leading to misunderstandings, conflicts, and hurt feelings. It's important to be mindful of the impact of gossip and to avoid spreading rumors or sharing information that could be harmful to others.*"Believe nothing of what you hear, and only half of what you see." – Proverb.*

Gossip / roumours is main seed of overthinking

Once, an elderly man spread rumors about his neighbor being a thief. Shortly after, a theft occurred in their neighborhood. The neighbor was arrested based on the rumors. But during the court trial, it was proven that the neighbor was innocent and not involved in the theft. The real thieves were caught by the police. The innocent neighbor was released from prison.
Feeling wronged, the innocent neighbor sued the old man for defaming him. In court, the old man argued that his words were harmless. The judge then asked the old man to write down his rumors on paper, tear them up, and scatter them on his way home.

The next day, the judge asked the old man to gather all the torn pieces of paper. The old man couldn't find them all, explaining that the wind had scattered them everywhere. The judge used this to show that just like the torn pieces of paper, the rumors had spread and couldn't be taken back, harming the neighbor's reputation.

The moral of the story is to be careful with your words because once spoken, they cannot be easily undone, and they can cause lasting harm to others.

Great minds discuss ideas; average minds discuss events; small minds discuss people

Highlights the role of gossip indirectly Eleanor Roosevelt suggests that the focus of conversation reflects the level of intellect and maturity.

In this context, gossip aligns with discussions about people, indicating a shallow focus on others' lives rather than meaningful ideas or topics. Great minds are occupied with discussing ideas, innovations, and concepts that contribute to progress and growth. Average minds engage in discussing events, such as what's happening in the world around them. On the other hand, small minds tend to gossip about individuals, often in a negative or trivial manner, without contributing to meaningful conversation.

Therefore, gossip, being associated with discussions about people, is depicted as a characteristic of small-mindedness, distracting from more significant and constructive discussions about ideas and innovation.

Gossip is the Devil's radio

George Harrison suggests that gossip spreads negativity and distraction much like a radio broadcasting harmful messages. In simple terms, gossip and rumors often fuel overthinking by circulating unverified or negative information about others, like a radio broadcasting bad news.

When people engage in gossip, they often overthink about others' lives, making assumptions and judgments based on incomplete or false information. This constant chatter can lead to unnecessary worry and anxiety, consuming valuable mental energy. Therefore, Harrison's quote implies that gossip, like a radio spreading negativity, can fuel overthinking and distract us from more important matters.

Gossip is poison. Gossip is like cancer. It hurts, but then it spreads

Taylor Swift's suggest the Gossip or roumers are one of the main source of Overthinking , further he quoted "Gossip is poison. Gossip is like cancer. It hurts, but then it spreads," emphasizes the harmful nature of gossip and its similarity to cancer.

In simple terms, gossip is compared to poison because it spreads negativity and harm. Like cancer, gossip starts small but then spreads rapidly, causing pain and damage along the way. When people gossip, it hurts not only the ones being talked about but also those spreading it and even those listening to it.

Overthinking often accompanies gossip because it encourages dwelling on negative or untrue information, leading to unnecessary worry and stress. Swift's quote warns that gossip is not only hurtful but also contagious, spreading negativity like a harmful disease.Other experts they motivating the Overthinkers to comeup in their lifes

"Believe nothing of what you hear, and only half of what you see."

3. A art of creating problems that weren't there.

Overthinking is something many people experience. It is the act of thinking too much about something, worrying over details, and imagining negative outcomes that might never happen. Overthinking can turn simple decisions into complicated puzzles and make us feel stressed and anxious.

Overthinking plays a significant role in this context. When we overthink, we become paralyzed by our thoughts, constantly analyzing and reanalyzing situations without taking any concrete steps. This leads to inaction and missed opportunities. For example, we might overthink a job opportunity so much that we never apply, or we might dwell on a personal conflict without ever addressing it, letting it fester and worsen. On the other hand, acting without thinking can lead to hasty decisions that we later regret. Impulsive actions without proper consideration can create new problems and complicate our lives.

Live Inspiration story

Simran Sharma: From Adversity to Champion

Simran Sharma, born in 1999 in Ghaziabad, Uttar Pradesh, is a visually-impaired para athlete. She was selected for the Indian team at the 2022 Asian Para Games in Hangzhou, China, where she won silver medals in the 100m and 200m T12 events.

Born prematurely after six and a half months, Simran faced vision impairment and spent over six months in an incubator. Growing up, she was teased by neighbors for her walking posture. However, she overcame these challenges and transformed her life through determination and resilience.

On a Saturday evening, Simran ran her personal best timing of 24.95 seconds in the women's 200m T12 final, becoming the world champion at the World Para Athletics Championship in Kobe, Japan.

Simran grew up in Goelpuri, Modinagar, with her father, Manoj Kumar, a medical practitioner, and her mother, Savita Sharma, who encouraged her to walk and run in the neighborhood park. This early encouragement helped her gain confidence, and she began competing in inter-college competitions.

In 2015, she met Gajendra Singh, who would become her husband and coach. Singh, an athlete himself, initially focused on building Sharma's strength before training her in sprints. They married in 2017 despite family resistance. Singh's support was instrumental in her training and success.

Two years after their marriage, inspired by para athlete Narayan Thakur, Simran decided to compete in the para category. She obtained her license for the women's T13 category in 2019 by participating in the World Para Grand Prix. To fund the license, the couple took a loan and sold a plot of land.

Simran won gold in China and qualified for the World Para Championships in Dubai, finishing eighth in the 100m T13 final. In 2021, she clocked 12.74 seconds in the 100m at the World Para Grand Prix in Dubai and qualified for the Tokyo Paralympics, where she finished fifth in the heats.

Despite suffering a thigh injury before the World Para Athletics Championships in Paris, Simran won silver medals in the Hangzhou Asian Games. She clocked 12.68 seconds in the 100m and 26.12 seconds in the 200m final.

Simran's journey from being teased to becoming a world champion is a testament to her perseverance and the unwavering support of her husband. Her story inspires many, showing that with determination and support, one can overcome any obstacle.

Most of the problems in life are because of two reasons: we act without thinking or we keep thinking without acting,

The quote, "Most of the problems in life are because of two reasons: we act without thinking or we keep thinking without acting," highlights how both impulsive actions and overthinking can create problems in our lives.

Overthinking plays a significant role in this context. When we overthink, we become paralyzed by our thoughts, constantly analyzing and reanalyzing situations without taking any concrete steps. This leads to inaction and missed opportunities. For example, we might overthink a job opportunity so much that we never apply, or we might dwell on a personal conflict without ever addressing it, letting it fester and worsen.

On the other hand, acting without thinking can lead to hasty decisions that we later regret. Impulsive actions without proper consideration can create new problems and complicate our lives.

The key is to find a balance: think things through enough to make informed decisions, but don't get stuck in a cycle of overthinking that prevents you from taking action.

The more you overthink, the less you will understand.

Habeeb Akande highlights how overthinking can cloud our judgment and lead to confusion rather than clarity. When we overthink, we often create problems that don't actually exist. We start imagining worst-case scenarios, misinterpreting harmless situations, and reading too much into minor details. This excessive thinking distorts reality, making it harder to see things clearly.

For example, you might overthink a simple comment from a friend, turning it into a sign of a hidden issue or conflict that isn't there. This imagined problem causes unnecessary stress and anxiety, preventing you from understanding the true nature of the situation. Instead of resolving anything, overthinking only creates more confusion and misunderstanding.

To avoid this trap, it's important to recognize when you're overthinking and take steps to clear your mind. Focus on facts, communicate openly with others, and take action based on reality, not imagined scenarios. This way, you can prevent unnecessary problems and gain a better understanding of your situations

Imagine you have a small problem, like choosing what to wear to a party. For most people, this is a simple decision. But if you overthink it, you start worrying about many things. What if you choose the wrong outfit? What if others judge you? What if the weather changes? These thoughts swirl around in your head, making a small decision feel huge and scary. This is the art of creating problems that weren't there.

Overthinking often comes from a fear of making mistakes or wanting to be perfect. We worry about all the possible outcomes and try to plan for everything. This can make us feel stuck, unable to make decisions. **For example, a student might spend hours worrying about an exam, thinking about all the things that could go wrong. Instead of studying effectively, they waste time and energy on their worries.**

Overthinking can also affect our relationships. If we overthink what someone said or did, we might imagine negative intentions that aren't real. For instance, if a friend doesn't reply to a message right away, an overthinker might worry that the friend is angry or doesn't like them anymore. In reality, the friend might just be busy. These imagined problems can cause unnecessary stress and conflict.

4. Fear of making Mistakes

The fear of making mistakes is a common experience that affects many people, hindering their ability to take action, make decisions, and fully enjoy life. This fear stems from various causes, including perfectionism, the fear of judgment from others, and concerns about the potential negative consequences of errors. As a result, individuals may experience procrastination, overthinking, and missed opportunities.

To overcome the fear of making mistakes, it's essential to embrace imperfection and recognize that mistakes are a natural part of the learning process. Instead of fearing them, mistakes should be viewed as valuable opportunities for growth and improvement. Positive thinking can help shift focus away from potential negative outcomes, while taking small steps allows individuals to gradually build confidence and reduce their fear. By adopting these strategies, individuals can confront their fear of making mistakes and lead more fulfilling lives.

The greatest mistake you can make in life is to be continually fearing you will make one

Elbert Hubbard's highlights the paralyzing effect of overthinking. When we constantly fear making mistakes, we tend to overthink every decision and action. This fear can lead to indecision, inaction, and missed opportunities.

Overthinking due to the fear of making mistakes creates a cycle where we become so preoccupied with potential errors that we fail to take any meaningful steps forward. This constant worry prevents us from learning, growing, and experiencing new things. Instead of viewing mistakes as learning opportunities, we see them as threats to be avoided at all costs.

Mistakes are proof that you are trying

This reminds us that making mistakes is a natural and important part of the learning process. When we make mistakes, it shows that we are putting in effort, taking risks, and pushing ourselves beyond our comfort zones. It is a sign of active engagement and a willingness to grow.

Instead of fearing mistakes, we should embrace them as valuable opportunities for improvement. Each mistake provides a lesson, teaching us what doesn't work and guiding us towards what does. By acknowledging our mistakes and learning from them, we become more resilient and better equipped to achieve our goals.

Failure is not the opposite of success; it's part of success." - Arianna Huffington

Often, people overthink because they view failure as the end of the road, something to be avoided at all costs. This fear of failure can paralyze them into inaction, preventing any forward progress.

Our greatest glory is not in never failing, but in rising every time we fail. - Confucius

The fear of making mistakes can lead to excessive rumination over past failures, creating a mental block that hinders future efforts. Overthinkers often dwell on their mistakes, unable to move past them.

Example: A student who failed a math test might overthink every mistake they made, worrying that they will never be good at math. This mindset can prevent them from studying harder for the next test. If they adopt the view that their true success lies in their ability to bounce back from failure, they can focus on improving rather than lamenting their past mistakes.

I can accept failure; everyone fails at something. But I can't accept not trying." - Michael Jordan

People often fear trying new things because they worry about failing. This leads to overthinking every potential outcome and never taking the first step.

A person who wants to start a business might overthink every potential risk and failure scenario. They might worry about financial loss, criticism, or market competition to the point where they never launch their business. By accepting that failure is a natural part of trying, they can push past their fears and take that crucial first step, understanding that not trying at all is a far greater failure.

"Success is not final, failure is not fatal: It is the courage to continue that counts." - Winston Churchill

Overthinkers might focus too much on the permanence of failure or success, fearing that a single failure could define their entire journey.

Don't be afraid to fail. Be afraid not to try." - Michael Jordan

Failure is a natural and necessary part of the path to success. Overthinking and fearing mistakes can hold you back, but embracing failure as a learning experience and continuing to try despite setbacks is what leads to true achievement. Don't have fear of failure.

5. Confused mindset

A confused mind says 'I don't know.' A peaceful mind says 'It doesn't matter.'"

When your mind is confused, you often find yourself saying, "I don't know," because you're unsure about what to think or do. But when your mind is peaceful, you say, "It doesn't matter," because you're okay with not having all the answers.

In simple words, when you overthink, you feel confused and uncertain about things. You keep questioning and worrying about every detail. But when you have peace of mind, you're okay with not understanding everything perfectly. You accept that some things are beyond your control, and you're fine with it.

Confused mind set story

In the heart of a lush forest, where sunlight filtered through the canopy of emerald leaves, there lived a gentle deer named Orion. Orion was known throughout the forest for his graceful leaps and his endearing innocence. But there was something peculiar about Orion—he possessed a fragrant navel.

It was said that every night as Orion slept beneath the starlit sky, his navel exuded a sweet, intoxicating fragrance that perfumed the air around him. The other forest creatures marveled at this phenomenon, attributing it to some mystical enchantment bestowed upon the deer by the forest spirits.However, what the animals didn't realize was that the fragrance emanated from within Orion himself. Deep within his being lay a reservoir of untapped talent, waiting to be discovered. But like the dear with its fragrant navel, Orion remained unaware of the extraordinary gift he possessed.

As Orion roamed the forest, he couldn't shake off a sense of restlessness and confusion. Despite the admiration he received from his fellow creatures for his external beauty and charm, he felt an emptiness gnawing at his soul. He yearned for something more, something beyond the superficial praise and admiration.One moonlit night, as Orion lay beneath the stars, his mind abuzz with questions and uncertainty, he heard a soft voice whispering in the gentle breeze. It was the voice of the wise old owl, Athena, who perched on a nearby branch, her luminous eyes gazing intently at the deer.

"Orion," she said in her melodious voice, "within you lies a talent so extraordinary, so wondrous, that even you are unaware of its existence."Orion's ears perked up at the owl's words, his heart fluttering with anticipation. With newfound determination, Orion embarked on a journey of self-discovery, delving deep into the recesses of his soul. He explored his passions, his dreams.He realized that true talent resided not in the external accolades and admiration of others, but in the depths of one's own being.And so, with his newfound wisdom and inner strength, Orion embraced his true self, sharing his gifts with the world and inspiring others to look within themselves to discover their own hidden talents.

Moral of the story is just like the dear with its fragrant navel, each of us holds within us a unique and extraordinary gift, Confusemind makes waiting to be uncovered and shared with the world. Identify internal talent and develop avoiding confusion mindset.

Sometimes you need to step back to see the bigger picture. Confusion is a state of mind where clarity is just around the corner." - Suzy Kassem

This quote means that when you're confused or unsure about something, it can help to take a step back and look at the situation from a broader perspective. When you're confused, it's like being in a foggy area where you can't see clearly. But if you give yourself some space and time, you might start to understand things better. Confusion is just temporary, and clarity is not far away.

Confusion is the first step towards clarity

This quote suggests that confusion is not necessarily a bad thing; it's the starting point on the journey to understanding and clarity. When you're confused, it means you're beginning to question and seek answers. By acknowledging your confusion and exploring it further, you can eventually find the clarity you seek.

6. Procastination and Self excuses are a one-way ticket of overthinking to nowhere

A "one-way ticket to nowhere" typically refers to a situation or decision that leads to a destination or outcome that is uncertain, undesirable, or without a clear purpose or direction. When we make excuses for ourselves, it's like buying a one-way ticket to nowhere. Self-excuses lead to overthinking, where we get stuck in our thoughts, constantly justifying why we can't do something. This cycle of overthinking prevents us from taking action and making progress. Instead of moving forward, we remain in the same place, trapped by our own doubts and reasons.

To break free from this, we need to stop making excuses and start taking action. By doing so, we can move past overthinking and begin to achieve our goals. Remember, the only way to get somewhere is to take the first step, not to sit and think of reasons why you can't.

Procrastination is the act of delaying or postponing tasks or actions that need to be done, often by focusing on less important or more enjoyable activities instead. This habit can lead to stress, missed deadlines, and a feeling of guilt or inadequacy. People procrastinate for various reasons, such as fear of failure, lack of motivation, or feeling overwhelmed by the task at hand.

An example of a "one-way ticket to nowhere" could be quitting a stable job without having another job lined up and without a clear plan for the future.

Imagine someone feeling unsatisfied and restless in their current job. Instead of carefully considering their options, they impulsively decide to quit on a whim, believing that leaving their job will lead to a better life. However, they haven't taken the time to search for new employment opportunities or consider the financial implications of being unemployed.

Without a job or a plan in place, they find themselves directionless and uncertain about their next steps. They may struggle to make ends meet, experience feelings of regret, and find it challenging to regain stability in their career and personal life. In this scenario, quitting their job impulsively without a clear plan represents taking a "one-way ticket to nowhere," as it leads to uncertainty and a lack of progress towards a meaningful goal.

7. Lack of self motivation

Motivation is like fuel for our lives. It's what drives us to do things, like working hard, studying, or pursuing our dreams. When we feel motivated, we have energy and enthusiasm to tackle challenges and achieve our goals.

Imagine you have a big test coming up. You know you need to study, but you feel tired. That's when motivation comes in. It's like a little voice inside you saying, "You can do it! Keep going!" With motivation, you find the strength to open your books, review your notes, and prepare for the test.Motivation is important because it helps us stay focused and determined. It gives us a reason to get out of bed in the morning and face the day ahead. Without motivation, life can feel dull and directionless. We might struggle to accomplish even simple tasks because we lack the drive to do them.Think about your dreams and aspirations. Maybe you want to become a doctor, travel the world, or learn a new skill. Whatever it is, motivation is what will help you get there. It's like a guiding light, pushing you forward and reminding you of what's possible.

In life, we encounter many obstacles and setbacks. It's easy to feel discouraged or give up when things get tough. But with motivation, we find the courage to keep going, to persevere even when the odds are against us.So, whether it's studying for a test, chasing your dreams, or simply gettIng through the day, motivation is essential. It's the spark that ignites our passion and propels us toward a brighter future.

Live Inspiration of Nirma – Karsan Bhai Patel

If you don't have motivation it causes for the Overthinking. Below mentioned inspiration story tells us don't get demotivate your self, bounceback the situations.*Karsanbhai Patel who lived in a small town in Gujarat, India. Karsanbhai worked as a lab assistant at a government research center, where he earned a modest salary.Karsanbhai Patel, the founder of Nirma, faced numerous challenges throughout his life but remained resilient and determined to overcome them. One of the most tragic events in his life was the loss of his beloved daughter, Nirupama.*

Nirupama was Karsanbhai's inspiration for naming his company Nirma. However, her untimely death due to an accident was a devastating blow to Karsanbhai and his family. Losing his daughter, who meant so much to him, left Karsanbhai heartbroken and in deep sorrow.Despite the immense grief he experienced, Karsanbhai found the strength to carry on. He channeled his pain into his work, pouring his energy into building Nirma into a successful business. Karsanbhai's determination to honor his daughter's memory and provide for his family drove him to overcome the challenges he faced.In the early days of Nirma, Karsanbhai encountered numerous obstacles. He had to compete with established detergent brands that had significant market share and financial resources. Additionally, he lacked the infrastructure and distribution network needed to reach a wider audience.

To overcome these challenges, Karsanbhai adopted a grassroots approach to marketing and distribution. He traveled from village to village, promoting Nirma detergent door-to-door and offering free samples to potential customers. His personal touch and dedication to quality earned the trust of consumers, and Nirma soon gained popularity across India.Despite facing skepticism and resistance from established players in the industry, Karsanbhai remained undeterred. He believed in the value of his product and was determined to make Nirma a household name.

Through self motivation, hard work, perseverance, and innovation, Karsanbhai gradually expanded Nirma's product line and market reach.

8. Lack of Tust

Trusting yourself is essential for personal growth and success. Believe in your abilities, intuition, and judgment. Embrace your strengths and weaknesses, knowing that mistakes are opportunities to learn and grow. With self-trust, you can overcome challenges, pursue your dreams, and navigate life with confidence and resilience.

Runouts in cricket often stem from two key aspects. Firstly, batsmen may fail to complete runs due to miscommunication or slow reactions. Secondly, a lack of trust between batting partners can lead to hesitation, resulting in runout dismissals. Effective communication and mutual trust are vital to avoid such costly errors on the field.

Trust is the confidence or belief in the reliability, integrity, and honesty of someone or something. Trust forms the foundation of healthy relationships, whether in personal, professional, or societal contexts.

Regarding the Trust, Jack Ma founder of Alibaba has quoted "When doing sales, the first people who will trust you will be strangers. Friends will be shielding against you, fair weather friends will distance from you. Family will look down upon you. The day you finally succeeded, paying the bills for every get-together dinner, entertainment, you will realised: everyone else is present except strangers.- Jack Ma"

People tend to trust you when they believe they are interacting with the real you (authenticity), when they have faith in your judgment and competence (logic), and when they feel that you care about them (empathy). When trust is lost, it can almost always be traced back to a breakdown in one of these three drivers.

"Whether your friends believe it or not, Whether your parents believe it or not.That's not important to you believe it, your team believe it and work day and night on this.That's how things happen" further he has quoted

" I didn't have a rich father. I tried three times for university, all failed. I applied for Harvard ten times, all failed; they didn't want to see me. For the last time, I went to the teacher's college, which was considered the third or fourth class of my city. So I applied for jobs thirty times, got rejected. It was so difficult at that time; I was so frustrated because I taught in the university; my pay was ten dollars a month. Because I could not find a good job, in 1994, I decided to do something called the internet, and 23 of my friends were against it; they said this is a stupid idea.

We have never heard about the internet, and you know nothing about computers. And I never thought I was smart. Nobody believed that I could be successful because everybody said, "Well, this guy thinks differently, thinks crazily. You know, they think about something that will never work." I tried to borrow 3,000 U.S. dollars from the banks; it took me three months, but I still couldn't get it. We talked to over 30 or 40 venture capitalists; everybody said no, forget it. A lot of people said Alibaba is a terrible model. As I said, I believed it. I thought this thing could be big. If we kept on working, I never thought it would be that big like today, but I believed that something, something was waiting for me out there, and I had to work hard to prove myself.

That was a tough experience. So we gathered 50,000 U.S. dollars from 18 founders. We started; for the first three years, we did not have even one dollar of revenue from our business. It's not easy; you don't make any money; you've got extraordinary claims, and yet you make nothing; that's the internet. Yes, but what's the point? Are you a millionaire? No, no. Do you want to be? Fun, well, I think, I hope. But why did we keep on going ahead, going forward? Because I received lots of emails of thanks from the customers; they said, "This is such a great thing; we cannot pay you, but this thing helped us. If you keep on helping us, one day you will be successful." And I believed this. Little by little, we built up our business; little by little, we built up our ecosystem of the infrastructure. And now, after 16 years, we have an Alibaba group, we have a Tmall group, we have a Taobao group, we have Alipay. And people say, "You are so smart.

How could you make a company like that?" Bill Gates, Warren Buffet, Jack Welch, Larry Page, Mark Zuckerberg, the difference between those people and other people is that they are always optimistic about the *future. They never complain; they always try to solve the problems of others. When you're optimistic, there is always opportunity. People say, "Where is the opportunity? I don't have a job; I don't have this; I don't have that." The best asset you have is that you are young. Don't complain; let other people complain. The opportunity always lies where people complain. Think about how you can make things different. When you think about it, start to do it.*

I saw a lot of young people with fantastic ideas every evening, but in the morning, they go to the office and do the same thing again. If you really want to be entrepreneurial, you have to do things before other people do; you have to wake up before other people wake up; you have to be braver than others. When I was young, I went to Hangzhou West Lake; there's a hotel, many foreign visitors visited there. And I went there every morning at five o'clock to practice my English. The foreign visitors came, and I practiced my English.

I don't know why at that time, but I found everything the foreign visitors told me was so different from the things my parents told me, my teachers told me, and the newspapers I read. So since then, I think about everything, use my own brain to think. To everybody, to any person, tomorrow is new.

Make the move, make the action. Whether investors believe in this or not, whether your friends believe it or not, whether your parents believe it or not, that's not important. You believe it, your team believes it, and work day and night on this. Make enough mistakes; you fall, you stand up. If you really want to work for yourself, think about others, because only when other people are successful, when other people are happy, you'll be successful, you will be happy. Don't worry about the money; money follows the people. People should follow their dreams. If you have a dream, just go ahead."

Frances Frei and Anne Morriss Trust model , May-June 2020, Harvard Business Review.Trust has three core drivers:

- ❖ Authenticity
- ❖ Logic
- ❖ Empathy

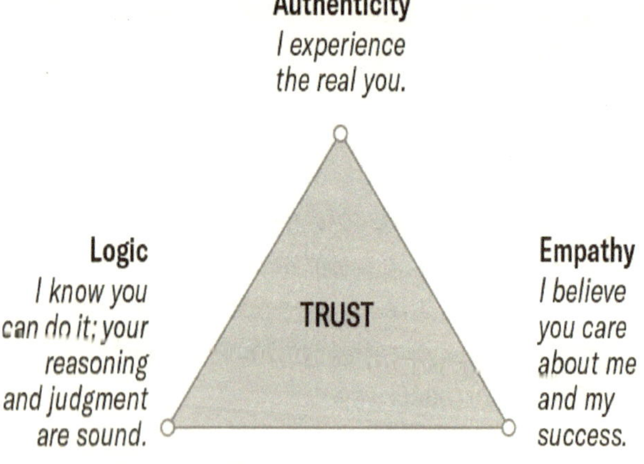

9. Self Doubt

Self doubt kills more dreams than failure ever will.~ Suzy Kassem

Self-doubt is the anchor that keeps our ships from sailing. It can prevent us from taking risks and seizing opportunities, ultimately holding us back from reaching our full potential. Don't let self-doubt hold you back. You are capable of more than you think. As William Shakespeare wisely noted, "Our doubts are traitors, and make us lose the good we oft might win, by fearing to attempt." This quote reminds us that doubt can betray our dreams and keep us from achieving success simply because we are too afraid to try. Trust in your abilities and take that leap of faith— you might be surprised at what you can achieve.

Don't have self doubt - Sundar Pichai, the CEO of Alphabet Inc and Google, emerged from humble beginnings in Tamil Nadu, India, to become a prominent figure in the tech industry. His journey reflects resilience and determination. Growing up, Pichai faced financial challenges and shared a room with others during his student life, but he never let this deter his focus.

Joining Google in 2004, Pichai's leadership and innovative mindset propelled him forward. Despite facing obstacles, he played a vital role in the success of Google products. As CEO, Pichai navigated significant changes and controversies with integrity and inclusivity.

Despite a near-miss opportunity for the CEO position at Microsoft, Pichai continued his journey with unwavering determination. His story teaches us not to doubt ourselves, even in the face of challenges. Sundar Pichai's path inspires us to persevere and believe in our potential, regardless of our beginnings.

10. Don't be over emotional

Overthinking can cloud your judgment. When we let our emotions take over, it's like having a foggy mind where it's hard to see things clearly. Overthinking makes simple decisions seem complicated and can lead to unnecessary stress and worry. Remember, it's important to pause, take a step back, and clear your mind before making decisions. Don't let your emotions overpower your ability to think rationally. Stay calm, trust yourself, and focus on finding solutions rather than dwelling on problems. Clear thinking leads to better decisions and a happier life."

Lesson from the Bharata Ratna Sachin Tendulkar

The incident involving Australian bowler Brad Hogg taking the wicket of Indian cricket star Sachin Tendulkar teaches us a valuable lesson:When Brad Hogg succeeded in dismissing Sachin Tendulkar, he celebrated excessively, capturing the moment with a photo of Sachin being bowled out and his own celebrations. Hogg then approached Sachin and asked for his autograph on the picture.

Sachin, displaying true sportsmanship, didn't let the dismissal affect him emotionally. Instead, he signed the photo with a message, "This will never happen again, Hoggy," indicating that Hogg would never take his wicket again. Sachin made it his mission not to get out to Hogg's bowling in his career.This incident teaches us not to be too emotional or overthink in the face of setbacks. Sachin's focus on his goal and his determination to bounce back stronger inspire us to stay focused on our objectives and overcome challenges with resilience and sportsmanship.

Emotions are like waves. You can't stop them from coming, but you can choose which ones to surf."

This quote beautifully captures the relationship between emotions and overthinking:When we're overwhelmed by emotions and thoughts, it's like being caught in a sea of waves. We can't control when emotions arise, but we can choose how to ride them. Overthinking often accompanies strong emotions, but we have the power to decide which emotions to focus on and which ones to let go.

Instead of being swept away by every wave of emotion or thought, we can choose to ride the waves that serve us positively. It reminds us that while we can't control everything that happens to us, we can control how we respond. So, let's choose to ride the waves of positivity and let go of overthinking and negative emotions that hold us back.

11.   Ego

More the knowledge, lesser the ego. Lesser the knowledge, more the ego." – Albert Einstein

Ego leads to overthinking . All of us know the big ships are designed to navigate through vast oceans and withstand fierce storms. They represent strength and resilience.

However, if a passenger creates even a tiny hole inside the ship, it can slowly take in water and eventually sink, that is called ego and overthinking. Similarly, our progress and achievements can be jeopardized by our own ego & overthinking. Just as a small hole can sink a mighty ship, unchecked ego& overthinking can undermine our success, ruin friendships, and damage relationships. Ego blinds us to our flaws, prevents us from accepting help, and makes us unwilling to compromise. To maintain progress and harmony, it's crucial to keep our ego in check, just as it's essential to repair any small hole in a ship to ensure it stays afloat. By fostering humility and self-awareness, we can prevent our ego from sabotaging our success and relationships.

Ego is just like dust in the eyes. Without clearing the dust, we can't see anything clearly." — Buddha

Ego is like dust in the eyes. If you don't clear the dust, you can't see clearly. When you have a big ego, you often think you are always right and better than others. This makes you overthink because you constantly worry about your image and what others think of you. You may replay past events, imagine future scenarios, and worry about being wrong or criticized. This constant thinking clouds your judgment and makes it hard to see things as they truly are. Instead of focusing on what's important, you get stuck in your own thoughts and miss the bigger picture. Clearing your ego, like clearing dust from your eyes, helps you see things clearly and focus on what really matters.

None can destroy iron, but its own rust can! Likewise, none can destroy a person, but their own mindset can."~Ratan Tata

Just as rust gradually eats away at iron, our negative thoughts and beliefs can corrode our mental strength and resilience. Our mindset plays a crucial role in determining how we perceive and respond to challenges, setbacks, and adversities. A positive and resilient mindset can empower us to overcome obstacles and thrive, while a negative mindset can hold us back and limit our potential.

Ultimately, it's not external forces that have the power to destroy us, but rather our own thoughts, attitudes, and beliefs. By cultivating a growth mindset, embracing challenges, and maintaining a positive outlook, we can safeguard our mental well-being and unlock our full potential.

Sigmund Freud model

Sigmund Freud, the founder of psychoanalysis, proposed a structural model of the human psyche composed of three distinct components: the id, ego, and superego.

Id: The id represents the primal, instinctual part of the psyche that operates on the pleasure principle, seeking immediate gratification of basic needs and desires, such as hunger, thirst, and sexual impulses. It is entirely unconscious and devoid of moral considerations or rationality.

Ego: The ego is the rational and conscious part of the psyche that mediates between the id, superego, and external reality. It operates on the reality principle, balancing the demands of the id with the constraints of the external world. The ego seeks to satisfy the desires of the id in socially acceptable and realistic ways, employing defense mechanisms to cope with conflicts between internal drives and external demands.

Superego: The superego represents the internalized moral standards, values, and ideals acquired from societal norms, parental influences, and cultural factors. It functions as the conscience, enforcing moral judgment, guilt, and self-criticism. The superego strives for perfection and moral purity, often imposing strict standards and expectations on the ego.

According to Freud, conflicts and tensions between the id, ego, and superego are inherent in human nature and can lead to psychological distress and neurotic symptoms.

"Less ego, more excellence. Less talk, more do. Less rude, more polite. Less fear, more wins." – Robin Sharma"

This quote by Robin Sharma highlights how reducing ego can lead to better outcomes in life. When you have less ego, you focus more on doing things well rather than showing off. This means you spend less time overthinking about your image or what others think of you. Instead, you concentrate on your actions and efforts, which leads to success. Talking less and doing more helps you achieve your goals without getting caught up in unnecessary thoughts. Being polite instead of rude fosters better relationships and reduces conflicts, making life smoother. Finally, having less fear and more courage helps you face challenges confidently, leading to more victories. In simple terms, the less you let your ego control you, the more you can achieve by focusing on what really matters.

12. Poor Relationships

The most important ingredient we put into any relationship is not what we say or what we do, but what we are." — Stephen R. Covey

Overthinking of youngstars and nuclear familes cause poor relations. It might be with Elderly parents, children, spouses. The statistics as are mentioned with industrialization and modernization, lifestyles have changed, leading to the breakup of joint families into smaller nuclear families. This has forced many elderly people to move from their homes to institutions or old age homes.

Relationship should be based on Understanding, and not on Adjustment!- Biplin Kumar GJ

The concept of old age homes is growing and becoming a necessity in today's Indian society. Recent data shows that there are more than 1,000 old age homes in South India alone. Currently, India's population of senior citizens has grown significantly from 5.6% in 1961 to 7.5% in 2011. Many elderly people in rural India are involved in unorganized agricultural work. Due to changing economic and social norms, the health and support for the elderly are becoming weaker. To address this, India recently started the National Program for Health Care of

Elderly (NPHCE) to improve healthcare infrastructure and train healthcare providers for elderly care.

A strong relationship starts with two people who are ready to sacrifice anything for each other.

Interms of Divorce "As of 2023, the divorce rate for first marriages is around 50%. For second and third marriages, the rates are 67% and 73%, respectively, for both men and women. The leading cause of divorce, cited in 75% of cases globally, is a lack of commitment. In the United States and Canada, 42% to 53% of marriages ended in divorce in 2023. Alcoholism contributes to divorce, with 34.6% of cases also involving abuse. The Philippines and Vatican City do not support divorce, while India has the world's lowest divorce rate. Countries like Japan, Argentina, Sweden, Spain, Mexico, Norway, and Slovenia have simplified divorce procedures, with Luxembourg having the highest divorce rate globally. Japan's divorce rate was 1.2% in 2023. Surprisingly, maids have a divorce rate of 26.3%. Divorce lawyers need seven years of education post-high school. Remarriages have a high likelihood of ending in divorce. Divorce rates in the U.S. rise seasonally, and higher education levels in women correlate with lower divorce rates.

Countries with the Highest and Lowest Divorce Rates

In 2023, the Maldives had the highest divorce rate, with 5.5 divorces per 1000 people. Other countries with high divorce rates per 1000 people include Guam (4.3), Russia (3.9), Moldova (3.8), Belarus (3.7), China (3.2), Aruba (2.9), Georgia (2.9), Ukraine (2.9), and Costa Rica (2.8). Conversely, the lowest divorce rates per 1000 people were observed in Vietnam (0.2), Sri Lanka (0.2), Peru (0.2), Saint Vincent and the Grenadines (0.4), Malta (0.5), South Africa (0.6), Ireland (0.6), Guatemala (0.6), Venezuela (0.7), and Uruguay (0.7).

It has been observed that suicide is the 4th leading cause of death among the late adolescent age groups (15–19 years) in India [4]. According to the NCRB, 2021 report, a total number of 10,730 adolescents (below 18 years of age) died due to suicides.

13. Excessive Interference in others Personal Matters

We live in an age when unnecessary things are our only necessities. ~Oscar Wilde

Over-involvement in others' matters can lead to numerous problems. When you become too involved in someone else's life, you might unintentionally overstep boundaries, leading to feelings of resentment and loss of trust. This behavior can also cause stress and anxiety for both parties. Instead of helping, it can hinder personal growth and independence. It's important to offer support and advice when asked, but also to respect the other person's ability to handle their own issues.

Helping others is noble, but meddling is just a nuisance

Helping others is a noble act, rooted in kindness and compassion. However, there's a fine line between genuine assistance and unnecessary interference. Meddling, although often well-intentioned, can lead to unintended consequences and disrupt the natural flow of events.

It's important to respect boundaries and allow individuals to navigate their own paths, making their own choices and mistakes along the way. While offering support and guidance can be beneficial, imposing one's opinions or solutions without invitation can be seen as intrusive and may hinder rather than help the situation. Ultimately, true assistance arises from understanding and respecting others' autonomy.

You don't have to share everything, speak about everything, brag about everything, argue about everything, and complain about everything. Some things are just meant to be kept for yourself. Royal Lradin

Excessive interference in others' personal matters often stems from overthinking. When we overthink, we create unnecessary worries and assumptions about others' lives. This can lead to an urge to control or "fix" situations that are not ours to handle. By overthinking, we imagine worst-case scenarios or believe we have the best solutions, prompting us to intrude where we're not needed. This behavior can strain relationships, as people may feel suffocated or resentful of the constant interference.

Intervening in others' lives often complicates rather than simplifies

Interfering in the lives of others can create more problems than it solves. While the intention might be to help or improve a situation, it can lead to unintended consequences and added complexity. Each person has their own unique circumstances and ways of dealing with challenges.

By imposing our opinions or solutions, we risk disrupting the natural flow and dynamics of their lives. It's important to recognize boundaries and respect the autonomy of others. Instead of intervening, offering support and guidance when requested allows individuals to maintain control over their own lives and decisions, ultimately leading to more effective outcomes.

Ankit Pandey says, ' Do Not Interfere Too-Much In Other's life B'coz Soon,You will loose Your's Self Respect.

It highlights the connection between overthinking and unnecessary interference. When we overthink, we often end up meddling in others' affairs, trying to control or fix situations that aren't ours to handle. This constant interference not only disrupts others' lives but also erodes our own self-respect. By focusing excessively on others, we neglect our own growth and peace.

"Not every battle is yours to fight. Learn to step back and let others handle their own affairs." — Unknown

It also frees us to focus on our own battles and personal development. Learning to distinguish which battles are truly ours to fight is essential for maintaining healthy boundaries and emotional well-being.

14. Habits

"Your beliefs become your thoughts,
Your thoughts become your words,
Your words become your actions,
*Your actions become your **habits**,*
*Your **habits** become your values,*
Your values become your destiny."
— Mahathma Gandhi

This quote by Mahatma Gandhi outlines the progression from beliefs to destiny, highlighting the pivotal role of habits in shaping our lives. It suggests that our beliefs influence our thoughts, which in turn shape our words and actions. As these actions are repeated over time, they become habits ingrained in our daily lives. These habits, in turn, reflect our core values, guiding principles that govern our behavior and decisions. Ultimately, these values determine our destiny, the culmination of our choices and actions over time. Therefore, the quote underscores the profound importance of cultivating positive habits aligned with our beliefs and values, as they ultimately steer us towards our desired destiny. It emphasizes the transformative power of habits in shaping the course of our lives.

Your habits determine your future. Successful people maintain positive habits, and they don't allow negativity to sabotage their efforts." - John Maxwell"

This quote means that the things you do regularly, your habits, can decide what happens to you in the future. Successful people usually have good habits, and they don't let negative things ruin their hard work. Instead, they stay focused on positive things and keep working towards their goals. So, if you want to be successful, it's important to have good habits and not let negativity stop you from achieving your dreams.

Overthinking habit, whether good or bad, can have various side effects depending on their nature and frequency.

Some common side effects of habits includeby over thinking:

- ❖ Negative Health Effects: Bad habits like smoking, excessive drinking, or poor diet can lead to health issues such as heart disease, obesity, and cancer.
- ❖ Decreased Productivity: Engaging in unproductive habits like excessive social media use or procrastination can reduce productivity and hinder goal achievement.
- ❖ Negative Impact on Relationships: Certain habits like being overly critical or neglecting responsibilities can strain relationships with family, friends, and colleagues.

- ❖ Financial Problems: Habits like overspending, gambling, or impulse buying can lead to financial stress, debt, and instability.
- ❖ Emotional Distress: Some habits, such as excessive worrying or self-criticism, can contribute to anxiety, depression, and low self-esteem.
- ❖ Physical Harm: Certain habits like nail-biting, hair-pulling, or excessive screen time can result in physical harm or discomfort.
- ❖ Social Isolation: Habits that involve withdrawal or avoidance, such as excessive gaming or substance abuse, can lead to social isolation and loneliness.

Regarding seven habits of highly effective people, The 7 Habits of Highly Effective People" by Stephen Covey outlines a holistic approach to personal and interpersonal effectiveness. Covey emphasizes principles such as proactivity, beginning with the end in mind, putting first things first, thinking win-win, seeking first to understand, then to be understood, synergizing, and sharpening the saw. These habits encourage individuals to take responsibility for their actions, set clear goals, prioritize tasks, communicate effectively, collaborate with others, and continually improve themselves. Covey's framework promotes a balanced and values-driven approach to life and work, helping readers cultivate habits that lead to long-term success and fulfillment.

15. Micro level comparision steals joy and is the enemy of your Happiness.

"Don't compare yourself with anyone in this world. If you do so, you are insulting yourself." — Bill Gates

I want to share a story about an unhappy crow. I hope it changes your life please don't compare yourselves.

There was a crow who was very sad because he was black. He cried a lot. One day, a monk saw the crow crying and asked why. The crow said, "I'm black, and no one likes black. No one wants a crow as a pet. I have to eat from the garbage. I hate my life."

The monk asked, "What would you like to be if you could change?"The crow replied, "I want to be a white swan. They are beautiful and peaceful."The monk said, "Okay, but first, meet a swan."The crow met a swan and said, "You are beautiful and must be happy."The swan replied, "Who said I am happy? I hate my white color. No one likes it. It looks like a coffin."

They went back to the monk, and the swan asked for a change too. The swan wanted to be a green and red parrot, admired by people. The monk agreed but asked them to meet a parrot first.The crow and swan found a parrot and praised it. The parrot said, "I'm not happy. My green color makes me hard to find in the jungle. I don't like it."

They returned to the monk, and the parrot asked to be a peacock. The monk agreed but told them to meet a peacock first. They found a peacock and admired its beauty. The peacock said, "I'm not happy. Hunters kill us for our feathers. Is that a good life?"

The crow asked the peacock, "Who is the happiest animal?" The peacock said, "You, the crow. No one hunts you. No one eats you. You are safe and free. You are the happiest bird."

The crow realized he was happy just as he was. The story teaches us to appreciate ourselves and not compare our lives with others.

"Don't compare yourself to others. There's no comparison between the sun and the moon. They shine when it's their time." — Unknown

Don't let the success of others discourage you. Let it inspire you." — Unknown"

This quote means that you shouldn't feel bad when you see others succeed. Instead of feeling sad or jealous, let their success motivate you to work harder and achieve your own goals.

Overthinking happens when you worry too much about others' achievements, which can make you feel discouraged. Micro-level comparison is when you constantly compare small details of your life with others, like their job, their house, or their relationships.

Instead of overthinking and comparing yourself to others, focus on your own path. Use others' success as a source of inspiration to improve yourself and reach your own goals.

Stop comparing yourself to others. You have your own race to run," reminds us that everyone has a unique path and journey in life.- Joel Osteen's

When you constantly compare yourself to others, it can lead to feelings of inadequacy and self-doubt. Overthinking these comparisons can make you forget your own strengths and achievements.

Instead, focus on your own goals and progress. Everyone's journey is different, and what works for someone else might not work for you. Remember, you are running your own race. Concentrate on your personal growth and celebrate your successes, no matter how small they might seem.

16.   Not being solution oriented

Overthinking is different from solving problems. When you overthink, you spend a lot of time worrying about the problem without trying to fix it. In contrast, problem-solving means looking for a way to resolve the issue.

For example, *imagine a storm is coming. If you are overthinking, you might say, "I wish the storm wouldn't come. It's going to be terrible. What if my house gets damaged? Why do bad things always happen to me?" This kind of thinking doesn't help you prepare for the storm; it just makes you feel more anxious.*

On the other hand, if you are problem-solving, you might think, "I will go outside and bring in anything that might blow away. I will put sandbags against the garage door to stop flooding. If the rain gets heavy, I'll buy plywood to board up the windows." This approach focuses on actions you can take to reduce the impact of the storm.

By concentrating on solutions rather than the problem itself, you can take productive steps to manage the situation and reduce your stress.

Chapter-III
Types of Overthinkers

Overthinking means thinking about something over and over again without finding any solution. It is a repetitive and unproductive way of thinking that makes you feel uncomfortable and stuck. Instead of solving the problem, you keep worrying about it, and it leads nowhere.

According to therapist Kimberly Martin, there are different ways overthinking can show up:

Rumination: This is when you keep thinking about negative thoughts and feelings repeatedly. For example, if you had an argument with a friend, you might keep replaying the argument in your mind and feeling upset about it, even though it's not helping you move on. This happens when you take one negative experience and apply it to all future situations. For instance, if you had a bad date, you might think, "I always have terrible dates" or "I'll never find a good partner." This leads to worrying about future events based on a single past experience, which might not be true.

Thinking or Not think -Hypervigilance:

This type of overthinking means seeing things as either all good or all bad, with no middle ground. For example, if you get some criticism at work, you might think, "I'm a complete failure," instead of recognizing that you did some things well but have areas to improve.

This is when you are always on the lookout for potential dangers. For example, if you are walking alone at night, you might keep looking around nervously, thinking about all the bad things that could happen, even if the area is safe.

Catastrophizing: This is when you assume the worst will happen. For example, if you have a job interview, you might think, "I'm going to mess up and not get the job," even though you haven't even had the interview yet.Overthinking in these ways makes it hard to find solutions and can make you feel more anxious and stressed.This is when you believe things are much worse than they actually are. For example, if you fear failing an exam, you might start worrying that you'll fail the class, then fail school, not get a degree, and end up jobless. This type of thinking makes you stress about the worst possible outcomes, even if they are unlikely.According to Martin, some emotions that can spark overthinking include:

- Nervousness
- Stress
- Sadness
- Excitement

Chapter-IV
Techniques to reduce overthinking

Technique is really personality. That is the reason why the artist cannot teach it, why the pupil cannot learn it, and why the aesthetic critic can understand it." — Oscar

Techniques to reduce overthinking are vital as they provide structured methods to regain control over thoughts, promoting mental clarity, peace, and productivity. These techniques empower individuals to break cycles of rumination, fostering healthier cognitive habits and enhancing overall well-being.

1. Awareness is the Beginning of Change
2. Mind your own business
3. Be solution focused
4. Change Negative thoughts
5. Think about what ca go right
6. Take Breaks
7. Practice self acceptance
8. Stop waiting perfection
9. Improve your Interpersonal skills
10. Stop comparing micro level comparision
11. Change your view of fear
12. Accept you are the Best
13. Notice when you are Overthinking
14. Be grateful

1. Awareness is the beginning of change

Before you can tackle your habit of overthinking, the first step is to become aware of it. This means noticing when you're starting to overthink. For instance, if you find yourself constantly doubting your decisions or feeling stressed, pause and recognize what's happening. Awareness is like a spotlight that helps you see the problem clearly.

Consider this quote by Lao Tzu: **"The journey of a thousand miles begins with one step."** Just like a long journey starts with a single step, overcoming overthinking starts with the simple act of noticing it.Another helpful quote is from T.S. Eliot: **"Every moment is a fresh beginning."** This reminds us that at any moment, you can choose to change. When you catch yourself overthinking, you have the power to shift your thoughts in a new direction.

For example, imagine you're worried about an upcoming presentation. Instead of spiraling into what-if scenarios, recognize that you're overthinking. This moment of awareness is your first step towards change. Take a deep breath, remind yourself that you've prepared well, and focus on one positive aspect, like practicing your opening line.

In that moment of awareness, you plant the seed for change, paving the way to a more mindful and less stressful approach to challenges.

2. Mind your own business

Those who mind don't matter, and those who matter don't mind." — Bernard Baruch

The quote "Those who mind don't matter, and those who matter don't mind." by Bernard Baruch means that the opinions of people who criticize or judge you are not important, while the people who truly care about you will accept you for who you are and won't judge you harshly.

Example: Imagine you decide to pursue a new hobby, like painting. Some people might criticize your paintings or think it's a waste of time. These people are the ones who "mind" and their opinions don't really matter. On the other hand, your close friends and family support you and encourage you to follow your passion, even if they don't fully understand it. These people are the ones who "matter" and they don't mind what you do because they care about your happiness.

The more you mind your own business, the less you will be minding other people's business.

It means that when you focus on your own life and problems, you won't have time or energy to get involved in other people's affairs.

Imagine you have a lot of schoolwork to do. If you concentrate on finishing your assignments and studying, you'll be too busy to worry about what your classmates are doing or gossiping about them. This helps you stay focused and productive.

Successful individuals focus on their own goals and don't concern themselves with others' actions.

Successful individuals focus on their own goals and don't concern themselves with others' actions. This means they concentrate on their own tasks, dreams, and progress instead of worrying about what other people are doing.

Example: Imagine a student named Sarah who wants to get top grades in her exams. She spends her time studying, doing her homework, and preparing for tests. She doesn't worry about how much time her friends spend on social media or how they study. By focusing on her own goals, Sarah stays on track and achieves her academic success.

Another example is an athlete training for a marathon. Instead of comparing themselves to other runners or getting distracted by their routines, the athlete sticks to their training schedule, diet, and goals. By doing this, they improve their performance and achieve their personal best.

3. Be fearless don't fear on your failures

The speech from Arnold motivating us to overcome from the overthinking and act.

Arnold Schwarzenegger's speech highlights his journey from a young bodybuilder to a successful actor and politician. He emphasizes the importance of having a clear goal and working tirelessly towards it. Despite the lack of money in bodybuilding, Arnold balanced college, construction work, rigorous gym sessions, and acting classes. He never wasted a minute, leading to his historic win as the youngest Mr. Universe at 20. He explains that without a vision, people drift aimlessly and end up in unfulfilling jobs.

Arnold describes the difference between him and others in the gym: while they saw working out as a chore, he saw it as steps toward his goal, making it enjoyable. He underscores the necessity of having a purpose, quoting Muhammad Ali's intense work ethic. Arnold debunks the myth of shortcuts to success, insisting on hard work and efficient time management.

He criticizes the concept of a "Plan B," arguing it dilutes the focus and commitment to "Plan A." Arnold stresses that fear of failure should not deter one from their goals. Citing Michael Jordan's missed shots, he illustrates that failures are part of the journey to success. The key is to get up after every fall, as winners persist despite failures. Arnold's message is clear: embrace failure, work hard, and stay focused on your goals without a fallback plan.

"Mistakes are proof that you are trying." - Unknown

This quote highlights that making mistakes is a natural part of effort and progress. To overcome overthinking, embrace your mistakes as evidence of your attempts and efforts. For instance, if you're anxious about presenting a project at work, remember that any errors you make are part of your growth process. Each mistake teaches you something valuable, helping you improve and succeed in the future. Instead of overthinking every potential error, recognize that mistakes are signs of progress and learning. This mindset shift reduces anxiety and encourages you to take action, knowing that trying is more important than being perfect.

"I have not failed. I've just found 10,000 ways that won't work." - Thomas Edison

Thomas Edison's perspective on failure teaches us to view unsuccessful attempts as part of the journey to success. When you overthink, you might fear failure and hesitate to take action. Instead, adopt Edison's approach by considering each failure a step closer to finding what works. For example, if you're developing a new product and face multiple setbacks, see each one as a learning experience. This shifts your focus from fearing failure to embracing experimentation, reducing overthinking and encouraging persistence. By understanding that failures are just steps in the process, you can maintain a positive outlook and continue moving forward.

"You build on failure. You use it as a stepping stone. Close the door on the past. You don't try to forget the mistakes, but you don't dwell on it." - Johnny Cash

Johnny Cash's quote advises us to use failures as learning opportunities without dwelling on them. To overcome overthinking, acknowledge your past mistakes but don't let them dominate your thoughts. For example, if you made a mistake in a previous relationship, learn from it and apply those lessons to future relationships instead of constantly worrying about repeating the same errors. By treating failures as stepping stones, you can focus on growth and improvement rather than getting stuck in a cycle of negative thinking. This approach helps you move forward with confidence and clarity.

"Your best teacher is your last mistake." - Ralph Nader

Ralph Nader's quote emphasizes learning from your most recent mistakes. To combat overthinking, analyze your last mistake to understand what went wrong and how you can improve. For instance, if you failed an exam, review your study methods and identify what didn't work. Use this information to adjust your approach for future exams. This proactive stance transforms mistakes into valuable lessons, reducing the fear of failure. By viewing mistakes as educational experiences, you shift your mindset from dwelling on errors to focusing on continuous improvement, thereby reducing overthinking and fostering resilience.

4. Be Solution-Focused

Overthinking is different from problem-solving. Overthinking is about dwelling on the problem, while problem-solving involves looking for a solution. Imagine a storm is coming. Here's an example that shows the difference between overthinking and problem-solving:

Overthinking: "I wish the storm wouldn't come. It's going to be awful. I hope the house doesn't get damaged. Why do these things always have to happen to me? I can't handle this." Problem-solving: "I will go outside and pick up everything that might blow away. I'll put sandbags against the garage door to prevent flooding. If we get a lot of rain, I'll go to the store to buy plywood so I can board up the windows." Problem-solving can lead to productive action. Overthinking, on the other hand, fuels uncomfortable emotions and doesn't look for solutions.

Visualization is another powerful technique. Envision the positive outcome of your actions. As Henry Ford said, "Whether you think you can, or you think you can't – you're right." Positive visualization helps to align your thoughts with productive actions, reducing anxiety.

Consider role models like Oprah Winfrey, who overcame a difficult childhood to become a media mogul. Oprah once said, "The greatest discovery of all time is that a person can change his future by merely changing his attitude." She exemplifies how shifting from overthinking to proactive problem-solving can lead to success. Oprah faced numerous challenges but focused on solutions, continually moving forward.

Another role model is Elon Musk, who tackles enormous challenges in technology and space exploration. Musk's approach is encapsulated in his quote, "When something is important enough, you do it even if the odds are not in your favor." Instead of overthinking the potential failures, he dives into problem-solving, turning visionary ideas into reality.

In summary, awareness is the first step to overcoming overthinking. Techniques like mindfulness, visualization, and breaking down tasks can shift your focus to problem-solving. By emulating role models like Oprah Winfrey and Elon Musk, who focus on solutions rather than dwelling on problems, you can lead a more productive and successful life.

5. Challenge Negative Thoughts

Overcoming overthinking from negative thoughts to positive ones involves questioning the validity of your negative thoughts. Here's how you can do it in simple terms:

First, ask yourself if the thought is true. Not every thought you have is a fact. Often, our minds create scenarios that aren't based on reality. When you catch yourself in a cycle of negative thinking, pause and challenge it. For instance, you might think, "I'm going to fail this project." Instead, ask, "Is this thought true? Do I have evidence to support it?"

Reframe Negative Thoughts Reframing means looking at a situation from a different perspective. When you catch yourself thinking negatively, try to find a positive angle.

"You miss 100% of the shots you don't take." — Wayne Gretzky This quote by hockey legend Wayne Gretzky reminds us that the fear of failure shouldn't stop us from trying. Focusing on what could go right encourages us to take action, knowing that inaction guarantees failure.

Serena Williams Serena Williams, one of the greatest tennis players, faced numerous challenges, including injuries and personal setbacks. Instead of thinking about what could go wrong, she focused on her goals and what she could achieve. Her mindset helped her win 23 Grand Slam singles titles. Serena's ability to reframe her thoughts and focus on her strengths has been crucial to her success.

You can't stop the waves, but you can learn to surf.

Jon Kabat-Zinn said, means that while you can't stop negative thoughts from coming, you can learn how to manage them. Instead of being overwhelmed, you can learn techniques to deal with these thoughts effectively.

Next, consider if there is evidence to support your negative thought. If you're thinking, "No one likes me," ask yourself, "Is there real proof of this?" Often, we find that our negative thoughts are based on assumptions rather than facts.

You are not a drop in the ocean. You are the entire ocean in a drop.

Rumi reminds us that we are much more than our negative thoughts. We have the capacity for great things and shouldn't let a few negative thoughts define us.Honore de Balzac said, *"When you doubt your power, you give power to your doubt. "* This reminds us that focusing on our doubts only makes them stronger. Instead, we should focus on our strengths and abilities.

Filling your mind with positive thoughts can lead to positive changes in your life. As an unknown author wisely said, "Your mind is a powerful thing. When you fill it with positive thoughts, your life will start to change." By replacing negative thoughts with positive ones, you can start to see changes in how you feel and act.

By applying these techniques and remembering these quotes, you can move from negative to positive thinking and manage overthinking more effectively.

6. Mental shift focus on the Positive Outcomes

Instead of dwelling on potential failures, think about the success you can achieve. This mental shift can transform anxiety into motivation.

"Don't think of what can go wrong, but what can go right." This quote encourages us to focus on positive possibilities rather than potential failures. By doing so, we can reduce anxiety and boost our confidence.

Inspiration Story: Michael Jordan Michael Jordan, one of the greatest basketball players of all time, missed over 9,000 shots in his career and lost nearly 300 games. He famously said, "I've failed over and over and over again in my life. And that is why I succeed." Jordan didn't focus on his missed shots or losses; instead, he focused on how each failure was a step toward success. His ability to see failure as an opportunity to improve helped him become a legend in basketball.

7. Visualize Success

Visualization is a powerful tool where you imagine the positive outcomes you want to achieve. This technique can build confidence and reduce overthinking.

"If you can dream it, you can do it." — Walt Disney This quote encourages us to visualize our dreams and believe in their possibility. By focusing on positive outcomes, we can inspire ourselves to achieve our goals.

Muhammad Ali Muhammad Ali, known as one of the greatest boxers, often used visualization techniques. He famously declared, "I am the greatest. I said that even before I knew I was." Ali visualized his success and believed in his greatness long before it was evident to others. This positive focus helped him overcome doubts and achieve extraordinary success in the boxing ring.

Learn from Mistakes and Move on Understand that mistakes are part of the journey to success. Learning from them rather than dwelling on them can help you maintain a positive outlook.

"The only way to prove that you're a good sport is to lose." — Ernie Banks This quote by baseball player Ernie Banks highlights the importance of learning from losses. Emphasizing growth and improvement from mistakes can help shift your focus from what went wrong to what can go right next time.

Kobe Bryant Kobe Bryant, the legendary basketball player, was known for his relentless pursuit of excellence. He said, "Everything negative – pressure, challenges – is all an opportunity for me to rise." Bryant used his mistakes and failures as opportunities to learn and improve, always focusing on how he could succeed in the future.

8. Relax yourself taking a breaks

Embrace Distraction and Positive Action

Overthinking can trap you in a cycle of worry and stress, preventing you from finding solutions and enjoying life. Instead of dwelling on a problem endlessly, try distracting yourself with positive and healthy activities. Engaging in activities like meditation, dancing, exercise, or learning an instrument can distance you from your worries, allowing your mind to relax and rejuvenate. For instance, instead of overanalyzing a disagreement with a friend, take a walk or start a new painting project. This break can help your brain work out a solution in the background.

Legend Swami Vivekananda emphasized the importance of positive action and focus. He said, "Arise, awake, and stop not till the goal is reached." Rather than getting stuck in the loop of overthinking, channel your energy into productive tasks that align with your goals.

Consider the example of a student preparing for exams. Instead of worrying about potential failure, they can take short breaks to engage in enjoyable activities like playing a musical instrument or gardening. These distractions not only provide relaxation but also allow their subconscious mind to process information and develop solutions.

Remember, sometimes your brain finds better ways to solve problems when you're not actively thinking about them. As the saying goes, "Sleep on it." Often, a good night's rest can bring clarity and fresh insights, showing the power of stepping back and letting your mind work in the background.

Don't let overthinking paralyze you. Distract yourself with positive activities, allow your mind to rest, and trust that solutions will come. Embrace the wisdom of legends and focus on taking constructive actions towards your goals.

9. Practice self acceptance

Overthinking often arises from dwelling on past mistakes or worrying about uncontrollable factors. To break this cycle, focus on cultivating self-acceptance and compassion. Research shows that individuals who practice self-compassion are more likely to adopt effective coping strategies.

Here are some strategies to help you become more self-accepting:

Practicing Gratitude: Regularly reflecting on the positive aspects of your life and the qualities you appreciate about yourself can shift your focus from negative thoughts to positive ones. For instance, start a gratitude journal where you write down three things you are grateful for each day. This simple practice can significantly reduce overthinking and increase your overall well-being.

Building a Support System: Surround yourself with people who provide encouragement and love. A strong support system can offer perspective and remind you of your strengths during times of self-doubt. Share your thoughts and feelings with trusted friends or family members who can help you see things from a different perspective.

Forgiving Yourself: Let go of past regrets by practicing self-forgiveness. Understand that everyone makes mistakes and that these experiences are opportunities for growth. For example, if you regret a decision you made at work, acknowledge the mistake, learn from it, and move forward without self-criticism.

"It's not the mistakes that matter; it's how you deal with them. The key is to not let them overpower your future." — Swami Sivananda

Swami Sivananda's wisdom encourages us to focus on how we respond to mistakes rather than the mistakes themselves. By adopting a mindset of learning and growth, we can prevent overthinking and move forward with confidence.

Overcoming overthinking requires a shift in focus from self-criticism to self-compassion. Practicing gratitude, building a supportive network, and forgiving yourself are powerful strategies to cultivate self-acceptance and reduce overthinking. Embrace these strategies to create a more positive and resilient mindset.

10. Stop Waiting for Perfection

"Done is better than perfect." — Sheryl Sandberg

This is a big one. For all of us who are waiting for perfection, we can stop waiting right now. Being ambitious is great but aiming for perfection is unrealistic, impractical, and debilitating. The moment you start thinking "This needs to be perfect" is the moment you need to remind yourself, "Waiting for perfect is never as smart as making progress."

Perfectionism often leads to overthinking, as you may constantly worry about every detail being flawless. This can prevent you from taking action and making progress. Instead, focus on making steady improvements and learning from each step along the way.

Consider the example of a writer working on a novel. If they wait for every sentence to be perfect, they may never finish their book. However, by allowing themselves to write imperfect drafts and revise later, they can make continuous progress and eventually complete their work.

"Strive for progress, not perfection." — Unknown

This quote emphasizes the importance of focusing on continuous improvement rather than an impossible ideal. Progress, no matter how small, is a step toward success.

"Perfection is the enemy of progress." — Winston Churchill

Winston Churchill highlights that the pursuit of perfection can hinder advancement. Embracing imperfection allows for growth and development.

"You don't have to be perfect to be amazing." — Unknown

Remember that excellence doesn't require flawlessness. Embrace your strengths and acknowledge that imperfections do not diminish your worth or capabilities.

Waiting for perfection is a common trap that leads to overthinking and inaction. By shifting your mindset to prioritize progress over perfection, you can overcome this barrier and make meaningful strides toward your goals. Embrace the journey of continuous improvement, and allow yourself the freedom to make mistakes and learn from them.

11. Improve Your Interpersonal Skills to Reduce Overthinking

*Knowing yourself is the beginning of all wisdom." —
Aristotle*

Improving your interpersonal skills can be a powerful way to curb overthinking. Studies have found that these skills have a significant impact on the habit of overthinking. Here are three key strategies to develop stronger interpersonal skills:

- Increasing self-awareness
- Boosting your self-confidence
- Practicing self-control

Increasing Self-Awareness:

*Believe you can and you're halfway there." — Theodore
Roosevelt*

Self-awareness is the foundation of effective interpersonal skills. By understanding your emotions, thoughts, and reactions, you can better manage how you interact with others. For example, if you notice that you often overthink after social interactions, take a moment to reflect on what triggers these thoughts. Are you worried about how you were perceived? By recognizing these patterns, you can work on addressing the root causes of your overthinking.

Boosting Self-Confidence:

Confidence plays a crucial role in how we communicate and interact with others. When you believe in your abilities and value yourself, you're less likely to second-guess your actions and words. One way to build self-confidence is by setting and achieving small goals. For instance, if you're nervous about speaking up in meetings, start by contributing one comment or idea per meeting. As you become more comfortable, your confidence will grow, reducing the tendency to overthink your participation.

Practicing Self-Control:

Self-control is strength. Right thought is mastery. Calmness is power." — James Allen

Self-control helps you manage impulsive thoughts and reactions, which can be particularly useful in preventing overthinking. Techniques such as mindfulness and deep breathing can help you stay calm and focused during interactions. For example, if you find yourself overthinking a comment you made in a conversation, pause and take a few deep breaths. This simple act can help you regain control and shift your focus away from unnecessary rumination.

Mahatma Gandhi is an excellent example of someone who exhibited exceptional interpersonal skills, self-awareness, confidence, and self-control. His ability to connect with people from various backgrounds, his unwavering belief in his principles, and his calm demeanor in the face of adversity were key to his success in leading India's independence movement. Gandhi's approach to communication and conflict resolution can inspire us to cultivate similar skills to reduce overthinking and enhance our interactions.

Developing stronger interpersonal skills through increased self-awareness, boosted self-confidence, and practiced self-control can significantly help in overcoming overthinking. Embrace these strategies and draw inspiration from leaders like Gandhi to lead a more mindful and balanced life.

12. Remember you are the best.- , don't overthink it;

Accept your best - Once you've given an effort your best, accept it as such and know that, while success may depend in part on some things you can't control, you've done what you could do.

Case Study: Google Founders vs. Yahoo

In the late 1990s, Larry Page and Sergey Brin, the founders of Google, faced tough competition from established search engines like Yahoo. Despite the challenges, they focused on innovating and providing the best user experience.

Larry and Sergey believed in their vision and didn't let doubts or overthinking hinder their progress. They famously said, "We are not thinking about making money; we are thinking about making a great search engine." This mindset allowed them to focus on their strengths and develop Google into the powerhouse it is today.On the other hand, Yahoo, once a dominant player in the search engine market, struggled to innovate and adapt to changing trends. Their then-CEO, Terry Semel, admitted, "I don't think we're in crisis, but we clearly need to work faster."Despite Yahoo's early success, their failure to keep up with Google's innovation and their tendency to overthink their strategies led to a decline in market share.

The case of Google founders vs. Yahoo illustrates the importance of believing in yourself and focusing on doing your best without overthinking. Like Larry and Sergey, trust in your vision and abilities, and accept that you've done your best. Success often comes to those who take decisive action and keep moving forward.

13. Keep moving Physical activities to beat overthinking.

When you catch yourself overthinking, it's time to get moving. Physical activity is a powerful strategy to overcome overthinking.When you feel trapped in overthinking, use that moment as a signal to engage your body:

✓ **Practical Movement:** Stand up, take a walk to another room, or do some house-cleaning. Simple physical tasks can help break the cycle of rumination and bring a fresh perspective.

✓ **Physical Health-related Movement:** Drink a glass of water or do some exercise. Hydrating and moving your body can shift your focus away from negative thoughts and boost your energy.

✓ **Joyful Movement:** Dance or wiggle around. Engaging in activities that bring you joy releases endorphins and lifts your mood, making it easier to combat overthinking.

Remember, when your mind is stuck, movement can set it free. So, get up, move your body, and let the physical activity guide you out of overthinking.

14. Embrace gratitude to conquer overthinking.

Gratitude can transform common days into thanksgivings, turn routine jobs into joy, and change ordinary opportunities into blessings." - William Arthur Ward

You can't have a regretful thought and a grateful thought at the same time, so why not spend the time positively? Every morning and every evening, make a list of what you are grateful for. Get a gratitude buddy and exchange lists so you have a witness to the good things that are around you.

Overthinking is something that can happen to anyone. But if you have a great system for dealing with it you can at least ward off some of the negative, anxious, stressful thinking and turn it into something useful, productive, and effective.

"Be thankful for what you have; you'll end up having more. If you concentrate on what you don't have, you will never, ever have enough." - Oprah Winfrey

This quote means that when you appreciate what you already have, you'll find more good things coming your way. But if you keep focusing on what you don't have, you'll always feel like you need more, and you'll never feel satisfied.

Gratitude is not only the greatest of virtues but the parent of all others. - Marcus Tullius Cicero

This quote means that being grateful is very important. When you are thankful for the things you have, it leads to having other good qualities like kindness, generosity, and happiness. Gratitude is like the root that grows other positive qualities in you.

15. Notice when you're overthinking.

"Notice the intricate details of life, and you'll find something worth living for." - Innocent Mwatsikesimbe

"Overthinking is a habitual thought pattern that is specific to you. For example, you may tend to overthink when you're home alone. If you notice that you've been by yourself in your room with spiraling thoughts for a while, it could be the first sign that you're overthinking—and the signal that you need to transition to one of your coping strategies.

"Being aware that you're overthinking is the first step to disrupting the behavior," says Siadat. "Ask yourself: What is usually the first clue that I've been overthinking?" she suggests. "Then the next step would be to identify what you would like to do instead."

You don't have to control your thoughts. You just have to stop letting them control you." - Dan Millman

This quote means that you don't need to try to forcefully control every thought that comes into your mind. Instead, you should focus on not letting your thoughts dictate your actions and emotions.

When you notice you're overthinking, it's like being aware that your thoughts are taking over and causing stress or anxiety. Instead of trying to stop every thought or control them all, you need to recognize that you have the power to choose how much attention and importance you give to those thoughts.

For example, if you catch yourself worrying about something that hasn't happened yet, you can acknowledge the thought without letting it consume you. By understanding that you don't have to let these thoughts control your feelings or actions, you can step back and decide how to respond more calmly and rationally.

16.   Aware of your patterns.

After you notice that overthinking is happening, start to practice mindful awareness. When you have the ability to tap into mindfulness, you can start to observe the full cycle of your overthinking pattern.

Ask yourself:

- What starts your overthinking pattern?
- How does it behave?
- How long does it take?
- Where do you feel it in your body?

Once you understand all the pieces of your overthinking pattern, you can get better at mindfully moving yourself out of your overthinking cycle.

Explanation: When you notice yourself overthinking, it's important to understand your patterns. Mindful awareness helps you observe your thoughts without getting caught up in them.

Example: Imagine Sarah notices she overthinks whenever she receives an email from her boss. She starts worrying about possible mistakes she might have made. By practicing mindful awareness, Sarah begins to recognize this pattern:

- **What starts her overthinking pattern:** Receiving an email from her boss.
- **How it behaves:** She starts imagining worst-case scenarios and feels anxious.

- **How long it takes:** She spends hours dwelling on it, affecting her productivity.
- **Where she feels it in her body:** She notices tension in her shoulders and a racing heart.

"You cannot control what goes on outside, but you can always control what goes on inside." - Wayne Dyer

This quote reminds us that while we can't always control external events, we have the power to control our internal reactions. Understanding our overthinking patterns allows us to regain control over our thoughts and reactions.

Japanese Panasonic Owner Struggle Story:

Take the story of Konosuke Matsushita, the founder of Panasonic. Despite facing numerous setbacks and failures in his business endeavors, Matsushita remained mindful of his own patterns and persisted. He said, "I learned a lot from failure. The more you fail, the more you learn. The more you learn, the closer you are to success."

Matsushita's ability to understand his own patterns of thinking and behavior allowed him to navigate challenges and eventually build one of the largest electronics companies in the world. His story illustrates the importance of mindful awareness in overcoming obstacles and achieving success.

Chapter-V

The Impact of Overthinking

1. Depression

Depression is a mental health disorder where a person feels extremely sad, hopeless, and loses interest in activities they once enjoyed. Overthinking plays a significant role in depression. People with depression often ruminate, which means they continuously think about negative events, their failures, or bad experiences. For instance, a person might overthink a minor mistake at work, replaying the event in their mind and imagining the worst possible outcomes, which only deepens their sadness and feelings of worthlessness.

Overthinking in depression can lead to a vicious cycle. The more a person thinks about their problems, the more overwhelmed they feel, and the harder it becomes to find solutions or take action. This can make them feel stuck and unable to improve their situation, increasing their feelings of despair.

For example, someone might repeatedly think about a breakup, constantly analyzing what went wrong and blaming themselves, which prevents them from moving on and finding happiness.

2. Anxiety

Anxiety is characterized by constant worry and fear about everyday situations. Overthinking is a common symptom of anxiety, as people with this disorder often dwell on potential problems and worst-case scenarios. For example, a person might overthink an upcoming presentation at work, imagining all the ways it could go wrong, which makes them feel extremely nervous and stressed.

Overthinking in anxiety can cause physical symptoms like a racing heart, sweating, and trouble sleeping. The constant worry can be exhausting and interfere with daily life. For instance, someone might spend hours overthinking a social event, worrying about what to wear, what to say, and how others will perceive them. This can make them avoid social situations altogether, which can lead to isolation and loneliness.

3. Generalized Anxiety Disorder (GAD)

Generalized Anxiety Disorder (GAD) involves excessive, uncontrollable worry about various aspects of life, such as health, work, and relationships. Overthinking is a core feature of GAD, as people with this disorder tend to worry about multiple things at once and find it difficult to stop. For example, someone with GAD might overthink their financial situation, constantly imagining losing their job or not being able to pay bills, even if there is no immediate threat.

Overthinking in GAD can lead to physical symptoms like muscle tension, headaches, and fatigue. It can also affect concentration and decision-making, making it hard to focus on tasks. For instance, a person might spend so much time worrying about their health that they can't concentrate on their work, leading to decreased productivity and increased stress.

4. Obsessive-Compulsive Disorder (OCD)

Obsessive-Compulsive Disorder (OCD) is a condition where a person has unwanted, intrusive thoughts (obsessions) and feels compelled to perform certain actions (compulsions) to relieve the anxiety caused by these thoughts. Overthinking is a major part of OCD, as individuals often get stuck on specific thoughts and can't let them go. For example, someone might obsessively worry about germs and repeatedly think about getting sick, which leads them to wash their hands excessively.

Overthinking in OCD can be very distressing and time-consuming. It can interfere with daily activities and relationships. For instance, a person might spend hours each day checking if they've locked the door or turned off the stove, overthinking the possibility of a break-in or fire. This can make it difficult to focus on other important aspects of life.

5. Panic Disorders

Panic Disorder is characterized by sudden, intense episodes of fear known as panic attacks. During these attacks, a person might experience racing thoughts, which can make the situation feel even more overwhelming. For example, someone having a panic attack might overthink their symptoms, such as a racing heart or shortness of breath, and believe they are having a heart attack, which increases their fear and panic.

Overthinking in panic disorder can also lead to anticipatory anxiety, where a person worries about having another panic attack. This can cause them to avoid certain places or situations where they've had attacks before. For instance, someone might avoid driving after having a panic attack in the car, fearing it will happen again. This can limit their activities and reduce their quality of life.

6. Post-Traumatic Stress Disorder

Post-Traumatic Stress Disorder (PTSD) occurs after experiencing or witnessing a traumatic event. Overthinking is common in PTSD, as individuals often replay the traumatic event in their minds and struggle to move past it. For example, a person who survived a car accident might constantly think about the crash, imagining different ways it could have been avoided or worrying about it happening again.

Overthinking in PTSD can lead to flashbacks, nightmares, and severe anxiety. It can make it difficult to focus on the present and enjoy life. For instance, a veteran with PTSD might overthink their experiences in combat, leading to insomnia and hypervigilance. This can affect their relationships and ability to function in daily life.

7. Social Anxiety Disorder (SAD)

Social Anxiety Disorder (SAD) involves intense fear and anxiety in social situations. Overthinking is a key feature of SAD, as individuals often worry excessively about being judged or embarrassed in front of others. For example, someone with SAD might overthink a conversation they had at a party, worrying that they said something stupid or that others didn't like them.

Overthinking in SAD can lead to avoidance of social situations, which can result in isolation and loneliness. It can also cause physical symptoms like sweating, trembling, and a racing heart. For instance, a student with SAD might overthink giving a presentation in class, worrying about making mistakes and being laughed at, which can lead to skipping the class altogether.

8. Attention Deficit Hyperactivity Disorder (ADHD)

Attention Deficit Hyperactivity Disorder (ADHD) is characterized by patterns of inattention, hyperactivity, and impulsivity. Overthinking can occur in ADHD, especially when individuals struggle to focus on a single task and their thoughts race from one topic to another. For example, someone with ADHD might overthink a homework assignment, jumping from one idea to another without being able to concentrate and complete the task.

Overthinking in ADHD can lead to feelings of overwhelm and frustration. It can also affect productivity and organization. For instance, a person with ADHD might overthink their daily schedule, getting stuck on planning every detail and feeling paralyzed by the number of tasks they need to complete. This can make it difficult to get started on any task and lead to procrastination.

9. Bipolar Disorder

Bipolar Disorder is a mental health condition where a person experiences extreme mood swings, including manic (high) and depressive (low) episodes. Overthinking often occurs during manic episodes, where thoughts can race uncontrollably. For example, during a manic phase, a person might overthink their plans and ideas, jumping rapidly from one thought to another and feeling overly optimistic and energized.

During depressive episodes, overthinking can take the form of rumination, where individuals dwell on negative thoughts and feelings. For instance, someone might overthink their past mistakes and feel overwhelming guilt and sadness. This can make it difficult to function and find motivation to do everyday activities.

10. Agitated Depression

Agitated Depression is a severe form of depression characterized by restlessness, irritability, and agitation, rather than the typical lethargy seen in depression. Overthinking is common in agitated depression, as individuals might constantly worry and feel anxious. For example, someone with agitated depression might overthink minor issues, feeling restless and unable to relax.

Overthinking in agitated depression can lead to physical symptoms like pacing, fidgeting, and an inability to sit still. It can also cause irritability and difficulty concentrating. For instance, a person might overthink a disagreement with a friend, feeling angry and upset, and replaying the argument in their mind. This can lead to strained relationships and increased emotional distress.

11. Medication Side Effects

If someone experiences overthinking as a side effect of medication, it's important to consult a doctor. The doctor might adjust the dosage or prescribe a different medication to alleviate these symptoms. For instance, if a person starts experiencing racing thoughts after taking a new antidepressant, their doctor might switch them to a different medication that doesn't have this side effect.

Chapter-VI

Therapies

<u>Warning</u>: Therapies are done under supervision of medical practitioners only. No reader should do any of the therapy on their own. These therapies are mentioned for orientation purposes only. Self-medication is harmful. The author and publication are not responsible for any such actions.

Therapies to Overcome Overthinking Disorders. There are several therapies for the application. Few therapies are mentioned below.

1. Cognitive Behavioral Therapy (CBT)

CBT is a therapy that helps people identify and change negative thought patterns and behaviors. Here's how it works step-by-step:

1. **Identify Negative Thoughts:** The therapist helps the person recognize their negative thoughts. For example, Sarah believes she will fail at work tasks.
2. **Challenge These Thoughts:** The therapist encourages Sarah to question the evidence for her beliefs. Are her thoughts based on facts or assumptions?
3. **Replace with Positive Thoughts:** Sarah learns to replace negative thoughts with more realistic,

positive ones. Instead of thinking she'll fail, she thinks about her past successes.

4. **Behavioral Changes:** The therapist helps Sarah change her behaviors that stem from negative thoughts. She might start setting small, achievable goals to build confidence.

Example: Sarah fears she will mess up a presentation. Through CBT, she learns to challenge this thought by recalling successful presentations she's given before, reducing her anxiety.

2. Mindfulness-Based Stress Reduction

MBSR helps individuals stay present and reduce overthinking through mindfulness practices. Here's the process:

1. **Mindfulness Training:** Learn mindfulness techniques such as deep breathing, meditation, and body scans.
2. **Practice Regularly:** Set aside time daily to practice these techniques, focusing on being present in the moment.
3. **Apply in Daily Life:** Use mindfulness in everyday activities, like eating or walking, to stay present and reduce overthinking.

Example: John feels anxious about future events. By practicing mindfulness, he learns to focus on the present moment, reducing his anxiety about things that haven't happened yet.

3. Exposure Therapy

Exposure therapy gradually exposes individuals to feared situations to reduce anxiety and avoidance. Here's how it works:

1. **Identify Fears:** The therapist and person identify the specific fears causing anxiety.
2. **Create Exposure Plan:** Develop a plan to face these fears gradually, starting with less intimidating situations.
3. **Gradual Exposure:** Begin exposing the person to the feared situation in a controlled way, increasing exposure over time.
4. **Build Tolerance:** Through repeated exposure, the person learns to tolerate and reduce anxiety.

Example: Emma is afraid of elevators. She starts by looking at pictures of elevators, then standing near one, and eventually riding in one with the therapist's support.

4. Medication

Medication can help manage symptoms of overthinking disorders. Here's the process:

1. **Consultation:** Visit a healthcare provider to discuss symptoms and get a prescription.
2. **Follow Dosage:** Take the medication as prescribed, regularly and at the same time each day.
3. **Monitor Effects:** Keep track of any side effects and report them to the healthcare provider.
4. **Regular Check-ups:** Have regular follow-ups with the provider to adjust the dosage if needed.

Example: Mike takes an antidepressant to manage his overthinking related to depression. With regular use and monitoring, his symptoms improve.

5. Dialectical Behavior Therapy

DBT focuses on emotional regulation and coping mechanisms. Here's the step-by-step process:

1. **Learn Skills:** DBT teaches skills in four areas: mindfulness, distress tolerance, emotion regulation, and interpersonal effectiveness.
2. **Apply Skills:** Practice these skills in daily life to manage emotions and reduce overthinking.
3. **Therapy Sessions:** Attend regular individual and group therapy sessions to reinforce skills.

4. **Ongoing Practice:** Continuously use these skills to handle emotional challenges.

Example: Rachel uses DBT techniques like deep breathing and positive self-talk to manage her intense emotions and reduce overthinking.

6. Acceptance and Commitment Therapy

ACT encourages acceptance of thoughts and feelings while committing to positive behavior changes. Here's how it works:

1. **Acceptance:** Learn to accept negative thoughts and feelings without trying to change them.
2. **Mindfulness:** Practice staying present and aware of thoughts and feelings without judgment.
3. **Values Clarification:** Identify personal values and what matters most.
4. **Commitment to Action:** Take actions aligned with these values, despite negative thoughts and feelings.

Example: Alex learns to accept his anxious thoughts and focus on engaging in activities that align with his values, like spending time with family.

7. Psychoeducation

Psychoeducation increases understanding of the disorder and teaches coping strategies. Here's the process:

1. **Education:** Learn about the disorder, its symptoms, and causes.
2. **Coping Strategies:** Learn techniques to manage symptoms, such as relaxation exercises and problem-solving skills.
3. **Support:** Receive support and encouragement from the therapist.

Example: Lisa learns about her anxiety disorder and practices deep breathing and time management techniques to reduce overthinking.

8. Support Groups

Support groups provide a space to share experiences and receive support from others facing similar challenges. Here's how they work:

1. **Join a Group:** Find a local or online support group for your specific disorder.
2. **Regular Meetings:** Attend regular meetings to share experiences and learn from others.
3. **Mutual Support:** Offer and receive support and encouragement from group members.
4. **Learn Strategies:** Learn coping strategies and tips from others who have similar experiences.

Psychometric Test & Evaluation

The Hamilton Anxiety Rating Scale (HAM-A) is a widely used clinician-rated scale designed to assess the severity of anxiety symptoms. Below are its key psychometric parameters and evaluations:

Purpose and Usage

- **Main Purpose:** To assess the severity of anxiety symptoms.
- **Population:** Adults, adolescents, and children.
- **Administration Time:** Approximately 10–15 minutes.

Structure

- **Items:** 14 items, each defined by a series of symptoms.
- **Domains:** Measures both psychic anxiety (mental agitation and psychological distress) and somatic anxiety (physical complaints related to anxiety).
- **Scoring:** Each item is scored on a scale from 0 (not present) to 4 (severe), with a total score range of 0–56.

Psychometric Questions

1. **Anxious Mood** -Worries, anticipation of the worst, fearful anticipation, irritability.

   ☐ 0 - Not present ☐ 1 - Mild ☐ 2-Moderate
   ☐ 3 - Severe ☐ 4 - Very severe **Score [   ]**

2. **Tension**-Feelings of tension, fatigability, startle response, moved to tears.

   ☐ 0 - Not present ☐ 1 - Mild ☐ 2-Moderate
   ☐ 3 - Severe ☐ 4 - Very severe **Score [   ]**

3. **Fears** -of dark, of strangers, of being left alone, of animals, of traffic, of crowds.

   ☐ 0 - Not present ☐ 1 - Mild ☐ 2-Moderate
   ☐ 3 - Severe ☐ 4 - Very severe **Score [   ]**

4. **Insomnia** -Difficulty in falling asleep, broken sleep, unsatisfying sleep and fatigue on waking, dreams, nightmares, night terrors.

   ☐ 0 - Not present ☐ 1 - Mild ☐ 2-Moderate
   ☐ 3 - Severe ☐ 4 - Very severe **Score [   ]**

5. **Intellectual-** Difficulty in concentration, poor memory

   ☐ 0 - Not present ☐ 1 - Mild ☐ 2-Moderate
   ☐ 3 - Severe ☐ 4 - Very severe **Score [   ]**

7. **Depressed Mood** Loss of interest, lack of pleasure in hobbies, depression, early waking, diurnal swing.

☐ 0 - Not present ☐ 1 - Mild ☐ 2-Moderate
☐ 3 - Severe ☐ 4 - Very severe **Score [ ]**

8. **Somatic (Muscular)** Pains and aches, twitching, stiffness, myoclonic jerks, grinding of teeth, unsteady voice, increased muscular tone.

☐ 0 - Not present ☐ 1 - Mild ☐ 2-Moderate
☐ 3 - Severe ☐ 4 - Very severe **Score [ ]**

9. **Somatic (Sensory)** -Tinnitus, blurring of vision, hot and cold flushes, feelings of weakness, pricking sensation.

☐ 0 - Not present ☐ 1 - Mild ☐ 2-Moderate
☐ 3 - Severe ☐ 4 - Very severe **Score [ ]**

10. **Cardiovascular Symptoms** -Tachycardia, palpitations, pain in chest, throbbing of vessels, fainting feelings, missing beat.

☐ 0 - Not present ☐ 1 - Mild ☐ 2-Moderate
☐ 3 - Severe ☐ 4 - Very severe **Score [ ]**

11. **Respiratory Symptoms** -Pressure or constriction in chest, choking feelings, sighing, dyspnea.

☐ 0 - Not present ☐ 1 - Mild ☐ 2-Moderate
☐ 3 - Severe ☐ 4 - Very severe **Score [ ]**

12. **Gastrointestinal Symptoms** -Difficulty in swallowing, wind, abdominal pain, burning sensations, abdominal fullness, nausea, vomiting, borborygmi, looseness of bowels, loss of weight, constipation.

☐ 0 - Not present   ☐ 1 - Mild   ☐ 2-Moderate
☐ 3 - Severe   ☐ 4 - Very severe **Score [   ]**

13. **Genitourinary Symptoms** -Frequency of micturition, urgency of micturition, amenorrhea, menorrhagia, development of frigidity, premature ejaculation, loss of libido, impotence.

☐ 0 - Not present   ☐ 1 - Mild   ☐ 2-Moderate
☐ 3 - Severe   ☐ 4 - Very severe **Score [   ]**

14. **Autonomic Symptoms**-Dry mouth, flushing, pallor, tendency to sweat, giddiness, tension headache, raising of hair.

☐ 0 - Not present   ☐ 1 - Mild   ☐ 2-Moderate
☐ 3 - Severe   ☐ 4 - Very severe **Score [   ]**

15. **Behavior at Interview** -Fidgeting, restlessness or pacing, tremor of hands, furrowed brow, strained face, sighing or rapid respiration, facial pallor, swallowing, etc.

☐ 0 - Not present   ☐ 1 - Mild   ☐ 2-Moderate
☐ 3 - Severe   ☐ 4 - Very severe **Score [   ]**

Psychometric Test Evaluation

Evaluation and Explanation of Anxiety and Overthinking Using HAM-A

The Hamilton Anxiety Rating Scale (HAM-A) is used to assess the severity of anxiety symptoms, including overthinking. It rates symptoms across various domains such as mood, tension, fears, insomnia, and somatic complaints. The evaluation of the scores is categorized into severity levels that help clinicians understand the extent of a patient's anxiety.

Severity Levels:

- ✓ <17 indicates mild severity
- ✓ 18–24 indicates mild to moderate severity
- ✓ 25–30 indicates moderate to severe severity

Mild Severity (<17)

A score below 17 suggests mild anxiety. Individuals may experience some anxiety symptoms but these do not significantly impair their daily functioning.

Example:Jane often finds herself worrying about her job performance. She occasionally feels tense and finds it slightly difficult to concentrate on tasks. However, she manages to complete her work and maintains a normal social life. Her HAM-A score of 15 reflects these mild symptoms of anxiety.

Mild to Moderate Severity (18–24) :-

Scores in this range indicate that the anxiety symptoms are more pronounced and may start to interfere with daily activities and quality of life.

Example: Tom frequently experiences restless nights due to racing thoughts about potential future problems. He often feels overwhelmed by minor issues and has a persistent sense of dread. His work performance is affected because he struggles with concentration and has started avoiding social gatherings. His HAM-A score of 22 falls into the mild to moderate severity range, indicating that his anxiety and overthinking are beginning to impact his daily life.

Moderate to Severe Severity (25–30)

A score between 25 and 30 suggests significant anxiety symptoms that substantially disrupt daily functioning and quality of life.

Example: Lisa's overthinking is pervasive and intense. She constantly fears that something terrible will happen, leading to frequent panic attacks. She struggles with severe insomnia, experiences physical symptoms like chest pain and shortness of breath, and finds it difficult to leave her house. Her HAM-A score of 28 indicates moderate to severe anxiety, demonstrating how her overthinking severely affects her ability to function in daily life.

References

- Harvard Business Review
- Harward Health news letters
- Educational podcosts
- Seminars
- Literature reviews
- Hamilton M.The assessment of anxiety states by rating. Br J Med Psychol 1959; 32:50–55.
- Maier W, Buller R, Philipp M, Heuser I. The Hamilton Anxiety Scale: reliability, validity and sensitivity to change in anxiety and depressive disorders. J Affect Disord 1988;14(1):61–8. Borkovec T and Costello E. Efficacy of applied relaxation and cognitive behavioral therapy in the treatment of generalized anxiety disorder. J Clin Consult Psychol 1993; 61(4):611–19
- Frances Frei and Anne Morriss Trust model , May-June 2020
- Sigmund model

Thank you

Dr. Y. Narasimha Raja